THE DIAMOND WEALTH REAL ESTATE SYSTEM

A simple guide to building a cash-flowing portfolio without quitting your day job

PETER DIAMOND

DEDICATION

To my amazing wife, Kayleigh—you are a constant motivation and inspiration. Your positive energy, dedication to family, and guidance and support are unmatched. I am truly blessed to have you as a partner.

You had my back from the very beginning when we had negative net worth, and you've never given up on us as we've grown to infinite wealth. Our relationship is the best investment I've ever made, as we build our love and life together.

P.S.

. . . and it doesn't hurt that you're so hot!

CONTENTS

INTRODUCTION

"More money has been made in real estate than in all industrial investments combined. The wise young man or wage earner of today invests his money in real estate."—Andrew Carnegie

Chained to the Desk

You have a great life. The goals you've had so far—you've achieved them all.

You have a good job, a partner or spouse, maybe kids. You have a mortgage on your single-family home, and you never miss a payment. You may even have a solid 401(k), slowly building equity for retirement. To the outside world, you're a true success.

But you want more. You have no assets outside of your primary house and company retirement savings. You won't be leaving anything significant behind for your kids or anyone else. You're stuck earning a wage, trading your time for money, giving your best to your employer.

You are lucky if you work only nine to five, and you spend most of your time looking forward to your next vacation. At the end of the day, someone else controls your wealth, time, and money. They decide if you get promoted, how many hours you work, and how you spend your days.

You have no control over your time, income, wealth, retirement, or life in general. You may make a lot of money, but you don't have the time to enjoy it. You are chained by golden handcuffs.

You feel the rumblings for more. You want to be in a situation where you're no longer chasing money. Instead, you want to be chasing everything that comes along with it: freedom, control, and a lifestyle you don't just tolerate, but love.

Does your kid need to be picked up at one o'clock in the afternoon? You want the flexibility to be there. Does your spouse have a big event next Tuesday? You want to drop everything and support them. You want to take off months at a time with your family. Or live a mobile lifestyle. Or save generously for retirement. Whatever it is, you want to live your dream.

You have the energy to go for more, but you have no idea how to get it. Stocks and bonds are out of your control and go up and down unpredictably with market fluctuations. Cryptocurrencies don't come with cash flow, and most banks have yet to recognize or lend against them. IRAs tend to be slow to appreciate. You are looking for a way out.

A Proven System

Real estate provides the answer: it gives you flexibility, financial stability, and freedom. When you invest in real estate, you make money on cash flow, and your properties continue to appreciate over time. You can create lasting assets for the next generation and passive income for your retirement, all without quitting your day job. And with proper structure, the return on investment for real estate is better than any other asset class in the world.

Real estate works, but you need to know the smart way to do it—a way that creates passive, unlimited, infinite wealth.

Traditional real estate investing isn't the answer. It requires huge amounts in hard capital. You need 20–25 percent just for the down payment, plus cash for repairs and renovations and holding and closing costs. Even if you can scrape the capital together for one deal, you're strapped when it comes to the next. You can't scale the system when you're relying on huge investments of your own cash, and you certainly can't save yourself to retirement.

That is why I created a system that has proven itself time and time again. The Diamond Wealth Real Estate System is much faster and more accessible than traditional methods of purchasing real estate, and it's proven to generate riches. It leapfrogs traditional ways of investing that require a lot of money for down payment, rehab, and closing costs. Because of the costs, conventional investing is out of reach for most starting investors.

More important, the Diamond Wealth Real Estate System turns traditional real estate investing on its head with my unique Cash-to-Buyer Twist. Instead of costing you money, it pays you money to purchase real estate.

The system I pioneered is so simple you can do it as a side hustle—though it's probably one of the best-paying side hustles in the world! You don't have to quit your regular job. You can keep your day job while building a passive income portfolio that ultimately can pay you forever.

If you are already in the real estate game, doing it part time, you can multiply your growth and create a portfolio faster than the traditional ways. If you're a wholesaler—someone who contracts with home sellers to buy their homes and then assigns those contracts to other investors—you can use this system to keep the best houses to generate infinite wealth, while wholesaling the rest for quick cash.

This system works even for full-time wholesalers who want a way to build long-term wealth with an asset that compounds value on its own.

Let's talk big picture. Why did I focus on single-family residential real estate when I created the Diamond Wealth Real Estate System? Real estate provides seven ways to generate revenue. One, right from the close, costs you nothing out of your pocket to purchase the property, but actually puts money *in* your pocket. This is the Cash-to-Buyer

Twist method in my system. Two, your tenant's rent, once refinanced, pays down the mortgage, growing the equity. Three, the rented properties give you predictable cash flow, month after month, like clockwork. Four, as the property depreciates each year, you write off the taxes, essentially giving you tax-free income, as the expense doesn't cost you anything out of pocket.

Five, market growth means the property increases in value over time—it appreciates. This means that the real estate compounds passively, without requiring your time, unlike a wage-earning job. Six, when you sell the property, you can roll the profits into more deals, all tax free, while deferring the gains. The wealth becomes infinite. Last, you can refinance and cash out against the value of the property, getting additional hard cash. The best part of the seventh way to make money is that the cash you receive is not a taxable event, as it's a loan against the asset.

No other asset class operates on all seven axes of wealth building, providing flexibility and helping you build cash flow. That's the beauty of real estate. Plus, you get to pass your wealth on to future generations without ever paying taxes, as you can defer them in perpetuity. Now that's generational wealth! And it's an excellent hedge against inflation.

The Diamond Wealth Real Estate System makes it even sweeter, because you do it with a unique Cash-to-Buyer Twist strategy that pays you to buy properties. You're no longer paying money to acquire investment properties. It's paying you.

The whole system—from purchase to infinite returns in a duplicatable, scalable process—is what I call the Diamond Wealth Real Estate System.

Your Real Estate Dream

This system works.

Using the Diamond Wealth Real Estate System, I bought my first property without any of my own capital. In a little over two years, I acquired twenty properties with market value—also known as after-repair value (ARV)—on the portfolio worth over $7 million, all while maintaining my full-time professional career.

Plus, I earn monthly cash flow. As of 2022, my portfolio brought in over $20,000 in passive cash flow every month. As I add more properties, my passive cash flow continues to grow.

What if you could start by bringing in even just $1,000 to $10,000 extra in passive income every month, while maintaining your current job or even reducing your hours? Would that give you a life you want?

Each home I buy becomes a perpetual source of income, through rent and other cash-flow pathways. I still work full time at the accounting/consulting firm I founded, but now I do so with the flexibility I always dreamed of.

And I do it while spending only a few hours a week on real estate.

If I want to leave the office at 1:00 p.m. to pick up my kids from school, I can. If I want to take a vacation with my family, while still earning revenue from my real estate investments, I can. It's not just my revenue I have control over; it's also my time, which I value more than the revenue. Your main goal should involve taking control of your time, not chasing the money. Having money without the time to use it to get the lifestyle you want is useless—and depressing. When you go for control of your time, on the other hand, the money will follow.

What if you had the time you wanted to spend with your loved ones? To do what you want and go where you want? Would that change your life?

When I first started out, I made a lot of mistakes. Now that I've done the hard work to overcome those mistakes, you don't have to repeat them. The blueprint in this book will help you avoid those missteps and get on the right track from day one.

If you follow the Diamond Wealth Real Estate System, you will have the knowledge you need to take control of your time, generate wealth outside of your wage-earning job, and build your own compounding assets—all while using little of your own capital. Each of those assets will then provide you with seven ways to continue generating infinite wealth.

Anyone can become a successful real estate investor, from the comfort of their desk, just by following these simple strategies. The deals shared in this story are real, but I have changed some names for confidentiality reasons.

One fun bonus this journey has given me: I got to name a street! I chose a name that represents the promise of this system in my life, and now in yours: Livin' the Dream.

This street is for you. With this system, you will be able to live your dreams and enjoy a lifestyle of freedom. You will have control over your wealth, time, and energy. You'll be livin' the dream.

Chapter 1

THE DIAMOND WEALTH REAL ESTATE JOURNEY

"Buying real estate is not only the best way, the quickest way, the safest way, but the only way to become wealthy."—Marshall Field

Traditional Investing Grind

The traditional way of building wealth is broken. You have one primary house—*if* you're fortunate enough to own a home. You probably rely on a 401(k)—which you have zero control over—to support you when you retire. You live for Fridays and the little vacations you take from the grind. Your annual increase in pay or occasional bonus is fixed, and there's not much you can do to increase it.

That is it. That's all you have.

Just put in your time in your job or corporate world and dream of retiring when you are sixty-five or older, hoping to have maybe a million or two in your 401(k) and your main residence paid off. That modest goal would be considered a success by most, but you know there should be more.

This system just doesn't work in the modern environment: you don't control your time, your money, or your assets.

You think you've already started to invest in real estate because you own your home, but contrary to popular belief, your primary home isn't an asset. Yes, its value goes up in time, but consider the repairs, remodels, and accessorizing: it's a financial black hole. It does nothing to bring you cash flow, and because it's probably the only house you have, you will make emotional decisions versus decisions based on income, every time.

If you sell, sure, your primary home becomes an asset. But then where do you live? You either move into a tiny condo or become a renter, neither of which you want. Even if you sell the house after it has appreciated, it's a great bonus to have some tax-free gains, but the only way you could turn that into an investment is if you downgrade or move somewhere else more affordable, and I know you don't want that.

It will be difficult to live the dream when *that's* all you have going on!

The Best Asset Class

Despite primary residence real estate being a liability, *investing* in real estate is the most lucrative of all asset classes. I mentioned this in the introduction chapter, but I want to give you more specifics here.

Real estate allows you to make money in seven ways, which I discuss in more detail in chapter 8:

1. **Cash flow:** The tenant pays rent, which you use to pay the principal, interest, taxes, and insurance (the PITI payment). The difference is your cash flow for the month, and this is the most direct way to make money from your properties.

2. **Principal paydown:** Every month, part of your mortgage payment is going toward paying down the principal of your loan. I like to think of this as a forced savings account, paid for by your tenant. Your net worth is going up each month.

3. **Appreciation:** Are the houses in your neighborhood getting cheaper? Likely not! The value of your properties will compound and appreciate over time, and when you sell, you can take advantage of the difference. With appreciation, you control an asset that grows and compounds over time. This is something you can never do in your current position,

which relies on your direct investment of time to generate income.

4. **Depreciation:** When you purchase a home, you can write off a portion of your total cost (called "basis") as an expense on your taxes. This expense goes against the income, providing you with tax-free cash flow. The best part is that in the basis calculations, the bank's money counts, so it doesn't even have to be your own money for the tax savings.

5. **Cash-out refinance:** As you pay down your principal and appreciate over time, the equity in your home goes up. Typically, most banks will lend you up to 75 percent loan to value. This is a great way to pull money out of the real estate. Best of all, it is a loan and not considered income for tax purposes. Borrowing against assets is an incredible way to access your net worth without triggering tax liability, since you are not selling or liquidating the asset.

6. **1031 exchange:** In time, every property will have too much equity, and the return from your current rental will no longer pencil out. When the cash-flow-to-equity ratio becomes disproportionate, you can sell your property and "exchange" it for a new one without paying capital gains tax. The gain is deferred, and, if properly structured, this can be

done in perpetuity. It's the best way to roll into more deals and scale your portfolio by deferring taxable gains. The basis and deferred gain calculation can grow extremely complex here, so consult with your tax professional before pulling the trigger.

As you can see, no other asset class allows for so many money paths and control. Cryptocurrency doesn't come with cash flow, while the small dividends you get from stocks are peanuts compared to what we're talking about through real estate. There is a time and a place for equities and cryptocurrencies, but neither of them depreciates, and you have no control over how they're managed and how much they'll appreciate. You certainly can't refinance your cryptocurrency to create more cash flow!

I am not saying you shouldn't diversify into other asset classes. However, residential real estate offers the control, flexibility, and so many ways to generate monthly cash flow and long-term, infinite compoundable wealth. The American Dream is alive and well, and the fastest way there for regular folks is through real estate—with the Diamond Wealth Real Estate System.

The Diamond Way

You'll notice I said there were seven money paths, but I only listed six. The Diamond Wealth Real Estate System offers you all the benefits I've described above, plus one final way to make money or enter the real estate game without using any of your own capital:

7. **Cash-to-Buyer Twist**: This is the key to paying nothing—or even being paid—to buy real estate. It's like a backdoor cash-out refinance, where you overfund your purchase with your initial loans, called hard money. The loan covers the cost of acquiring a property, plus extra to be returned to you at the close. This extra money can be used for renovations, cover holding costs, or go straight into your pocket as bonus cash. In some cases, you'll opt for no cash-out, but you still have bought the property with no money down, while participating in all the upside of owning real estate.

The Cash-to-Buyer Twist supercharges your cash position. You invest with little to no money out of pocket, *and* you get money back at the close. You literally get paid to buy, without the need for the 25 percent down payment traditional real estate investing requires. With this system, you're investing in real estate *without putting up any of your own cash as capital*. Unlike the traditional method, which is based on the initial purchase price, this system is based on the future ARV of the property.

You flip the traditional system on its head, buying the property outright with other people's money—that's the hard money loan—and then refinancing it with traditional banks. You pay off the private loan within months. Your investor makes money on interest payments, you get to keep the asset while spending little, *and* the property adds to your portfolio, bringing in cash flow that supports you in livin' your dream.

It is possible. I know because I've done it.

An Infinite Wedding Gift

The solution came to me from asking a single question.

In 2010, I proposed to my then-girlfriend, and she said yes. We started making wedding plans, but neither my fiancée's parents nor my parents could pay for the wedding. The beautiful wedding of our dreams was going to cost us over $50,000, and every penny was coming from us. So we started to save up.

Over the next year, as our bank account filled with cash and the date for putting a hotel deposit crept closer, we started to get cold feet about the big event. It was so much money! And there were so many other things we could do with that much cash in hand.

Finally, we sat down and talked it out.

"This is crazy," my fiancée told me. "Why waste all this money on a single day?" Her question set us on a new course.

She looked at me and declared, "I'd rather buy a condo."

At the time, condos in our area were going for less than our anticipated wedding cost, so the decision seemed like a no-brainer.

That got me thinking. "With what we've already got saved up," I said, "we can buy a condo *and* go on a two-week honeymoon to Mexico."

Her eyes lit up. "Having a paid-off home will help us build a life. A fancy wedding is just a one-day party. Plus, this way we still get a great trip!"

We agreed to elope.

Our first condo

We used $32,000 of our savings and bought a cute little condo outright in cash. Then we took an all-expenses-paid trip to Mexico. We went to Cabo, just the two of us. We got married the second day we were there and stayed for two weeks on our honeymoon.

The condo was a traditional starter home. It wasn't in the best neighborhood, but it did the trick, with two beds and one and one-half baths. Since we paid for it outright, we didn't have a mortgage, and our living expenses were low. This allowed us to pay off my student loans, enjoy life early on, and still set us on the right course for the future.

Our first house

After a few years, we moved into our first detached single-family house, using an FHA (Federal Housing Administration) loan, with a minimum down payment and a regular mortgage. At the time, I didn't know better, so we did pay private mortgage insurance. However, it still worked out. After a few years there, and some minor renovations to improve the value of the home, I was able to cash-out refinance the property and use the money to buy our second primary home. The first house then became a rental property.

When I saw how much the bank was willing to give us during the refinance of the house, I was amazed. We made back every penny of our down payment, plus all the renovation expenses, *and* walked away with an additional $55,000. In addition, since the refinance was a loan, we didn't pay any taxes on the transaction.

"This is incredible!" I thought. "Why sell the house when we could rent it out and keep building equity?"

Fast-forward to 2021, and this same house went through another cash-out refi of over $130,000. After the refi was done, the property still offered all the other benefits of real estate—just more proof that every property becomes its own infinite source of income. It's amazing what you can do with real estate.

Neon Lights

That moment changed our trajectory moving forward.

We moved into the new house, making the prior primary home our first properly structured rental (which in a way happened accidentally).

Neon lights went off in my head. "There has to be a way to scale this. How could I do the same thing with three, four, or even five properties?"

The sticking point was the down payment and rehab cost. We didn't have the cash to buy one property, let alone five!

I did the research, and before long I saw the answer. If I could find a way to borrow the initial purchase price, even at a high interest rate, I could do similar renovations, refinance at the new appraised value, and easily pay off the loan.

"Even better," I thought, "what if the initial loan for the purchase exceeds the purchase price, overfunding on the buy side and creating cash back at close?"

This way, my loan would cover some, if not all, of the repair cost. I would barely be out of pocket, or if I were lucky, even make money on the deal. Then, when the property was refinanced, it would all get paid back by the low interest rate the bank offers.

I didn't need to follow the traditional model of investing, which is hard to scale and extremely expensive. Using the traditional method, I might be able to buy only one rental property a year.

By overfunding the loan on the buy side, I created the foundations of a method to investing in real estate that put money in my pocket, created long-term cash flow, and was scalable.

THE CASH-TO-BUYER TWIST

I created the foundations of a new way to buy a property. I ended up with cash in my pocket and a system that was teachable, scalable, and infinite.

This Cash-to Buyer-Twist became the foundation of my Diamond Wealth Real Estate System.

When I discovered the infinite wealth generated through my system, everything changed. I realized I could secure a hard-money loan that covered the purchase price of a house, some repairs, and closing costs. Using that over-funded loan, I could fix up the property and then refinance it through a traditional lender at a much better interest rate. I would pay off my original loan and retain the real estate asset, providing flexibility and cash flow for life.

Other popular real estate investing methods ignore the issue of the purchase and, in the end, the bankability side; they assume everyone is capable of arranging a huge down payment, over and over again. They also assume everyone can easily refinance their way and then repeat the process. It sounds nice in theory but is extremely difficult for regular folks, especially if you're starting out with a limited budget. The Diamond Wealth Real Estate System completely sidesteps that problem, giving you the ability to live your life, work your job, and grow wealth *at the same time.*

Our decision not to have a traditional wedding bought us our dream. I often joke with my wife, "It's the wedding gift that keeps on giving!"

Our wedding gift became our infinite wealth path.

Your Journey to Infinite Wealth

I have used the same method ever since. It will serve you, just as it served me, to build your portfolio and start bringing in passive income every month. My main goal was always to have a second way of generating income and assets that would compound in value over time. This system allows you to keep your full-time job, while giving you more flexibility and freedom of choice.

Sure, you can find other real estate investing strategies out there, such as fix-and-flips, the buy-rehab-rent-refinance-repeat (BRRRR) method, holding notes, and more. But all require large down payments up front. The Diamond Wealth Real Estate System is the only one that allows you to purchase with no money out of pocket and maybe even cash back at the close using the Cash-to-Buyer Twist, while enjoying cash flow and all the other benefits of real estate mentioned earlier.

The Diamond Wealth Real Estate System allows you to keep working at your regular job. You can build a portfolio of cash-flowing properties while keeping your day job. In contrast, many other real estate strategies require your full-time attention. You practically have to quit your day job to do them. This simple system gives you time, flexibility, and income, while moving you toward freedom.

In time, if your cash flow is high enough to displace your current active wage income, you may take the leap into becoming a full-time investor. I prefer to keep my job and work part time, enjoying the flexibility of having monthly self-generating income while working—because I love to, not because I need to. Another reason you need to consider before deciding to quit is that your current day job is your bankability ticket. If you just quit, no bank will extend you a loan. You'll hear me talk a lot about bankability later in the book, as it's extremely important if you want to scale this model.

With this system, I focus on income-producing single-family residential properties. They offer the best flexibility and lendability, and they have the greatest market demand: everyone will always need a place to live! They are the best asset to start out in.

As we take a deeper dive, you'll discover five important elements of the infinite wealth system:

1. Identify the right market and know where to build your pocket.

2. Create deal flow and find the properties that will serve you best.

3. Access the money and get the loans you need.

4. Get the deal with a twist by ensuring your bank-ability and bring together the perfect team.

5. Implement a "buy-and-hold" strategy—the best one to increase your passive wealth.

Use this book as your guide. Read through the whole thing once, and then return to each chapter as needed, reminding yourself of the steps to take and the missteps to avoid. It can be your blueprint and your guide. Figure out what works best for you and find ways to adapt the lessons here to your own situation.

As you start on your Diamond Wealth Real Estate journey, remember to start small. Buy a single house and see it through to the end. Create small, quantifiable goals you can stick to. Even a single, properly structured income-producing property can be enough to change the trajectory of your life.

Once you read the book through once, you'll already be in good shape to begin your investment into infinite wealth.

You should also secure the services of a good legal and tax professional to help you with your deals (read more on building your team in chapter 7). The advice in this book is just that—advice. Always check the math and make your decisions with the advice of competent professional help, especially for your specific region.

The lessons I show you can apply in any geographic area in the United States, whether the market is hot or cold, and regardless of current interest rates. They also apply in any market, regardless of size or location. The principles are universal. I have coached many investors across the country on this method. It works like clockwork, regardless of the location.

At this time of writing, I primarily operate in Phoenix. The examples and numbers are from the Phoenix area, which, as of this writing, is one of the hottest and most competitive markets in the United States. If I can succeed in this competitive market, you can apply these principles and succeed anywhere you live.

Once you learn this system and start implementing it, you too will begin building your infinite wealth, one house at a time. With the Diamond Wealth Real Estate System, you'll be on your way to livin' the dream—your dreams.

Chapter 2

THE DIAMOND WEALTH FORMULAS

"If you don't own a home, buy one. If you own a home, buy another one."—John Paulson

Low Cost and Scalable

My investing discovery turned into possibility.

After I created the Cash-to-Buyer Twist, I realized I had discovered a way to overcome two obstacles to real estate investing: an expensive down payment and limited scalability.

I now had the bones of a method that put money in my pocket and was quickly scalable, turning the traditional real estate investing method on its head. After doing it over a dozen times, I had worked out the kinks to turn it into a consistent, repeatable, duplicatable system.

The Diamond Wealth Real Estate System offers a simple mathematical formula that pays you to purchase real estate and allows you to scale your real estate empire much more quickly than the traditional method. In this chapter, I show you an overview of the formula in action. As I go through subsequent chapters, I break down each step of the deal in more detail.

When you are starting out, capital preservation is key, which is why overfunding the loan on the front end is the preferred method of purchasing; you need to preserve your capital for the renovation and holding costs or the next project.

The last thing you want to be doing is putting a down payment on top of that. But in a traditional model, that's exactly what you have to do. You will have to provide, out of pocket, a 20–25 percent down payment of the purchase price. In addition, you have to come out of pocket for the repair and holding costs.

With my formula, you get paid to purchase the property each and every time.

Knowing Your Numbers

To know if a property is a good purchase, you'll need a handle on several numbers:

1. Estimated ARV & Diamond Cost Range (DCR)

2. All-in cost (purchase price, closing, holding, and rehab)

3. Initial loan amount

The ARV is the most important part of your real estate investing formula. This is the home value, after full repairs, based on recent comparable prices (or "comps") of sold houses in the area. If you go very aggressive, you can base your ARV on future appreciation, but this only works if you are in a very hot market. I recommend staying conservative at first, until you get a better handle on the process, especially if you don't have a lot of cash flow.

Next up is the DCR. For the deal to pencil, your all-in costs should never be more than 70–75 percent of the ARV. This is because you need a protection buffer in case the market fluctuates and your estimated ARV is wrong. Simply multiply your ARV by 70–75 percent to get your DCR. The lower your purchase price in comparison to your ARV, the better the deal.

Note that you can go over my recommended ARV thresholds—as high as 80 percent—but anything you go over will be out of your own pocket. As long as you know this going in, it's fine, but you don't want to be surprised by the amount. Keep in mind that even if you put your own out-of-pocket funds into the deal, you'll still benefit from huge savings over the traditional model.

Once you have the ARV and DCR, you need to gather four more numbers to decide whether the deal pencils: the purchase price, closing costs, holding costs, and rehab costs. Together, these costs make up your all-in cost.

1. The purchase price is how much you will pay for the property, including the price to the home seller *and any assignment fees to wholesalers* you may be working with. At this stage, you can also expect to pay an earnest deposit of $5,000 to $10,000, but since you get that money back when the deal closes, I don't include that figure in the formula.

2. Closing costs are the amount you pay the title/escrow company, as well as taxes, insurance, and other fees necessary to complete the purchase. On average, you can expect to pay $500 to $2,000 in closing costs.

3. Since a major part of the Diamond Wealth Real Estate System involves keeping this property for several months before you refinance, you need to know your holding costs. It typically takes about three to four months to rehab a property and refinance the hard money loan, so you need to be able to pay your costs during that period. Expenses include insurance, utilities, and loan interest.

4. The estimated rehab costs are how much the property will cost to renovate so you can refinance for the ARV. When calculating your renovation costs, be sure to include an "oops budget" for unexpected or over-budget expenses. That should be about 5 percent of the total repair costs. If you don't

use this much in repair costs, even better, but you're covered.

Add together your purchase price, closing costs, holding costs, and rehab costs to get your all-in cost.

With all of these numbers in hand, you're ready to learn how to buy a property with no money down.

The Cash-to-Buyer Twist Formula

With traditional real estate investing, you need to put in a large amount of money up front. It's impossible to buy a property and end up with money in your pocket.

The Diamond Wealth Real Estate System works completely differently. My twist is overfunding the purchase price with the initial hard money loan, renovating the property, and then refinancing with a traditional loan. This system is so unique because you base the initial loan on the future ARV instead of the purchase price. This model is the most unique and creative way to enter into real estate market. The Diamond Wealth Real Estate System is the only system that uses the future ARV to support your initial purchase.

With the twist, the hard money loan covers all or most of the renovations, so when you refinance out, you will have as little as possible tied up in the property. This can work down the line when you cash-out refinance, but it makes it that much better if you can do it from the beginning. Be aware that in a competitive market like Phoenix, where I invest, it is extremely difficult to fund repair costs up front. But in other, cooler markets, you may find it easier to do. Generally, my goal is to minimize the out-of-pocket expense and protect the capital, then refinance into a traditional loan later.

Number Review

It is important to have a strong handle on the formula, so let's review the numbers. First, determine the property's ARV. Then, calculate your DCR, which is 70–75 percent of the ARV.

Next, calculate your all-in cost:

$$\text{Purchase price} + \text{closing} + \text{holding} + \text{repairs}$$
$$= \text{all-in cost}$$

Finally, calculate how much of a loan you can take out based on the ARV.

Compare this number to the DCR to see if the deal pencils. If it does not, the difference will be out of pocket. This is okay as long as it's planned for. Even with some out of pocket, you will see tremendous savings over the traditional model of 20–25 percent down out of pocket.

The following is an example of an all-in cost that

works and uses the Diamond Twist to get you money back at close.

Example #1: Ideal example

Purchase price:		$100,000
Rehab:	+	$40,000
Closing costs:	+	$2,000
Holding costs:	+	$4,500
All-in cost:	=	$146,500

ARV:	$200,000
Loan at 70 percent:	$200,000 x 0.70 = $140,000
Loan at 75 percent:	$200,000 x 0.75 = $150,000

In this scenario, the initial loan at 75 percent will give you enough cash back to cover the total purchase price. Once repairs are done, you get a new loan to refi the $150,000 loan, giving you the house with nothing out of pocket.

Example #2: Realistic example

You won't always be able to buy a property with nothing out of pocket, but that doesn't mean it isn't still a good deal. Here's an example where you have to spend a little out of pocket, but you still save big compared to a traditional purchase.

Purchase price:		$100,000
Rehab:	+	$60,000
Closing costs:	+	$2,000
Holding costs:	+	$4,500
All-in cost:	=	$166,500

ARV:	$200,000
Loan at 70 percent:	$200,000 x 0.70 = $140,000
Loan at 75 percent:	$200,000 x 0.75 = $150,000
Out of pocket on 75 percent:	= $16,500

With this property, you can see that you have some out-of-pocket costs even at 75 percent. With the traditional model, you would have a $25,000 down payment plus $66,500 for rehab holding, giving you a total of $91,500 in costs, so the Diamond Twist method saves you big.

Infinite Return Calculations

With the Diamond Wealth Real Estate System, the returns are infinite. You can enjoy owning a single-family rental property with all the benefits and controlling an asset that grows in value, not only without having any money out of pocket, but also while getting paid to do it. When trying to quantify the returns, the numbers are simply too great: How do you quantify a return that doesn't cost you anything out of pocket? It is infinite.

Every house has the potential of providing you with infinite returns and scaling into infinite wealth. The best part about this system is that you are taking out a loan. It is not income; therefore, it will not trigger any income tax liability, as you are simply borrowing against your income-producing asset.

What is the first step in getting your first deal? Choosing your real estate pockets.

Chapter 3

IDENTIFY THE MARKET

"You're not just buying the house, you're buying the whole community."—Graham Salman

Bad Curb Appeal

In one deal, I bought a property completely sight unseen. After the deal closed, I went to see it, and I brought my wife with me. I pulled up in front of the house, and my wife let out a small sound of alarm: the house was in much worse shape than the initial pictures had suggested.

The paint was peeling off the walls, the roof was in terrible shape, windows were broken, and it didn't have air conditioning or a dishwasher. Across the street, the neighbors were sitting on their porch, tinfoil covering their windows; several cars parked in the front yard. Their music blasted so loudly it rattled our car windows. I turned the car off, and my wife looked at me in surprise.

"I can't believe we just bought this!" she said.

"It's not that bad," I promised.

Inside the house, she kept peering into bedrooms like she was afraid the ceiling would come down on her. "It's by far the worst one I've ever seen!" she said.

She was right—the place was a disaster! It had terrible curb appeal, and most buyers would walk right past. But I knew the neighborhood. I knew exactly how much the house would rent for, and I knew it would take only a little renovation to make it rentable.

"We don't have to live here," I reminded her. "It won't take marble countertops and a brand-new kitchen to make it appealing. A new coat of paint, a light remodel, and someone will love it."

I was right. We had our first tenant in the house just days after renovations were complete, and it was soon cash flowing over $900 a month with over six figures in equity—all because I knew my pocket, and I could see past the rocky outside to the strong bones underneath.

Time is always your best friend when it comes to real estate, and the house doesn't have to be up to your personal standards for someone to live in it. Once this house was fixed up enough to rent, it rented within days.

The trick to investing in real estate is identifying your market. When you balance a good pocket with a decent house (or a house with the potential to be decent if you can fix it up, or if you are optimistic about the area in the future because a big development is coming) and set high rental prices, you'll make back your investment every time.

Your Pockets

The first step to smart real estate investing is identifying your market. Your market is a combination of a specific location and a specific property type.

I prefer to start with an area I'm familiar with, so your local market or close to it is always a good start. You want to be in an area you're comfortable with—you have to know, or have a general idea of, what rents are going for so you can plan your investing strategy appropriately. While you don't need to invest in properties in your home city, your chosen area should be a place you know well.

I also prefer to choose two or three areas—I call them pockets—and cluster my investments there. Pockets are much smaller than cities: think on the scale of a single neighborhood.

Real estate books often will talk about "hot" and "cold" markets. In a hot market, housing prices are going up; in cold markets, housing prices are going down. Rather than focusing on what is hot or cold, look for markets with robust population growth, high-ranking universities, great hospitals, or growing industries like energy or technology.

The population demand alone will dictate much of the rent, making it more market resistant. Once you have the house properly structured, the value of the asset per se will not concern you; even if it drops by as much as 20 percent, rental decreases are rare in the developing markets, and your PITI (principal, interest, taxes, and insurance) payment is fixed (you can find the formula for calculating PITI in chapter 6).

To find out if a market is hot, watch population rates in your pockets. If population is rising, that means there's more competition for rent. If population is declining, rental rates won't be far behind—it's all about supply and demand for rental houses. You can use data from the census for population numbers, google the historical population rates, or pay for a service that can give you even more accurate income and population growth rates for your city.

Relocation trends also are a great indicator. You can find these on the U-Haul website or other online sites that track such data. Since COVID, remote work has been very popular, and high-taxed, high-restriction states have been unpopular. Follow the trends and see where people are moving to, as it could be a great opportunity to invest there.

Try to find areas that are likely to see growth or where industry is stable. Areas around universities and colleges are always good, because students want to be close to school, so even lower-class neighborhoods can demand high rent prices. also because cis I'm a big fan of hospitals and big developments, as employees want to live close to work. Big manufacturing areas and areas with stadiums are also good for this reason.

Do not focus on areas you would want to live in. I wouldn't walk my dog down some of the streets where I own houses! But I don't have to live there. I just have to be able to rent it out. Remember that it's an investment property, and treat it as such.

THE BEST POCKETS

My favorite pockets have these features:

- area in your home city or that you know well
- hot or stable markets
- growing population
- stable industries and job growth
- manufacturing industries
- universities, colleges, or schools
- large developments
- hospitals
- stadiums

Your neighborhood pockets do not have to have all these features—just enough to support a stable population of renters with stable incomes.

Once you know your pockets, you can hunt for properties by zip code. When you get leads, you'll know if it's in your area based on the zip. Then you can drill down to neighborhood pockets. I know my zip codes and watch for houses that come up in any of the zips. When a single-family home in the right price range comes up, I buy it sight unseen, every time. In chapter 4, I show you where to find those leads. For now, just know what areas you want to focus on.

Rent Levels Matter

If this is your first investment house, you're not going to know as much about real estate in your market, no matter how well you know the area. Counter this knowledge vacuum by doing your research. Go on Zillow, HotPads, Rentometer, or even Facebook Marketplace and check average rent prices for different properties in different neighborhoods.

Remember, there's a premium for dealing directly with the owner versus a management company, so the rent you charge can be higher than the rents you find on the other sites. Typically, I go 10–20 percent higher than the highest comparable I can find, and the method hasn't failed me yet.

To pick your market, look for a high ratio between selling prices of homes and rental prices. This is called the rent-to-cost ratio.

In a hot or competitive market, where you must act quickly to secure a property, you may not have time to check every expense of a deal. The rent-to-cost ratio gives you a shortcut.

If you are using Zillow, look at the Zestimate included on listings. You want the lowest Zestimate with the highest rent. In a normal market, you want the rent-to-cost ratio to be at least 1 percent. For example, if the Zestimate for a house is $100,000, you want the rent to be at least $1,000 per month.

In a cold market, the ratio could be much higher. In hot markets, that ratio often isn't possible, as the prices have increased much faster than the rents. If you are in a major market, you may have to settle for anything over 0.5 percent. Even with the lower ratio, you can still make the investment to yield great results.

If your rent-to-cost ratio is healthy, you will be cash flowing on your property regardless of whether the market goes up or down. You're buying based on what rent can support, and that will always leave you in solid shape.

Types of Properties

After you've chosen your area, you need to think about what kinds of properties you want to invest in. Your choice should be a mix of what makes you comfortable and what's popular in your local market. Since I'm not a full-time wholesaler, I like to go after houses that most investors pass on. For example, I like homes built in the 1950s and 1960s, brick-construction single-family houses in developing areas that need some love but demand higher rent. Often, they come with post-possession—when the previous owner stays in the house for a certain amount of time after the sale—or an extremely low-rent tenant whom you will need to incentivize to leave. By implementing this strategy, I have secured some great cash-flowing houses. It just takes more creativity to make them work.

Most of the "competition" or investors engaging in the real estate business full time go after the "stucco–tile" houses. These houses are typically built after the 1990s and have fewer issues to fix in the beginning. These are admittedly great to own, but they are much more expensive and extremely difficult to pencil for anyone who is not direct to seller. Typically, full-time wholesalers or real estate professionals are the only ones that can yield great returns on them.

Since I have a full-time practice and invest in real estate on the side, I had to get creative and find a pocket that yields the same benefits but requires a little more brainpower on the front end. I aim for houses with four or more bedrooms, or ones with the potential to become four bedrooms once rehabbed (I've noticed that rent is the best on larger properties, since they're harder to find). I also prefer units with decent yards and no homeowner associations.

With the larger homes and fewer restrictions, multigenerational families or large families can live in the house.

One reason we can command such high rents is because of this; the rent, in most cases, will be unaffordable for a single-wage earner, but with several incomes to cover the rent, it works. Most of my houses are occupied by large families where the parents and kids live under the same roof, and I've had great experiences with this.

Some investors stay away from multigenerational homes because they fear too much wear and tear, but the yields become much lower with smaller rents. If the rehab is done properly on the front end and everything is made to last—hardwood floors, no carpet, etc.—the house will be less likely to wear and tear, as the tenants can't hurt much. It should be mainly hassle-free for years to come.

It is rare to command maximum cash flow and maximum equity at the same time. Many of my peers who are doing similar investments get minimal or even negative cash flow at first, just to build the equity on the balance sheet. With my system, you can maximize both front-end cash flow and equity on the backside, from the beginning.

You do that by finding the lowest-priced house in a strong rental area, balanced against repairs the house will need to be rentable. If you're handy, you can do your own repairs, but if you're like me and sit behind a desk for a living, you'll need to hire the right people to make repairs for you.

And as simple as that—you have your market.

These are my criteria for investing:

- older houses
- single-family houses
- four bedrooms or potential for four bedrooms
- no homeowner associations
- large backyards

Regardless of what area or market you invest in, these types of properties appeal to the largest number of potential tenants.

Bad House, Good Pocket

For the reasons explained above, I often go for the dirtiest, most run-down property I can find, as long as it's in a neighborhood with a mix of nice and bad properties. Why? Because you'll get the best rate of return on the cost of your house versus the rent you can charge.

I live in one of the most competitive real estate markets in the country, Phoenix, so I have to think outside the box. The other wholesalers or investors have passed on most of the houses I get because of the state the house is in, the neighborhood, or a post-possession tenant. This works if you want zero headaches and have a ton of free cash you just want to park, but not if you're trying to build wealth while preserving your capital.

Instead, I've learned to see the diamond in the rough.

Remember the place from my example above? It looked like nothing—a dirt backyard, an empty, destroyed house, no A/C, no dishwasher, etc. It was hard for people to imagine building a life there, which meant less competition among buyers. People are visual: once you can present them with the finished product and amazing pictures, it'll rent every time. People just have a really hard time with the visions when all they see is a shack in need of repairs.

If you're smart and can see the bigger picture, like I did, you see how, with some work, you can fix up the house and make it not just livable, but able to command the highest rent in the neighborhood.

Always remember: it's a rental, not your primary home. People aren't looking for their dream home the way they are when they're buying. They're looking for something comfortable enough that checks their boxes. It's a very different mindset. You need to remove the personal thoughts, feelings, or desires you would apply to your primary house. Go in with the mindset that it is a rental, and you will be much more successful at it.

TIPS AND TRICKS

You understand your market. You've found a pocket. You're ready to learn to create deal flow. But before we move on, I want to remind you of these handy tips and tricks.

Get educated: You need to get outside of your bubble and see what else is out there. When you live in your nice house, with your nice job, you think that everybody needs to live like you. You will miss the opportunity unless you learn to look outside of your own experience.

Technology: Don't overlook the benefits of the technology available to you, most of it for free. I've mentioned Zillow; there's also Realtor.com and Redfin, among many others. These websites are not the only places to do research, but check them out, and find the right people and wholesalers to follow on social media. Most wholesalers love to showcase their success online, so they are easy to find. Once you find them, subscribe to their lists so you can receive the blasts when they have a new property.

Once you choose your pockets and types of properties to focus on, the next question is this: How do you find great deals that turn a good property into an excellent investment?

In the next chapter, you'll find four sources for finding golden deals.

Chapter 4

CREATE DEAL FLOW

"Business opportunities are like buses—there's always another one coming."—Richard Branson

A Friend and a Deal

I met my first real estate wholesaler through my professional network.

A friend of mine was a top real estate wholesaler. I had met him originally through professional events, but we clicked and became good friends outside of work. After my wife and I bought our first rental property, he approached me.

"Peter, I know you've been getting more interested in real estate lately. I was wondering if you'd be interested in a property that I have a contract on. I'm sharing it with you before I blast it out."

My friend showed me the property and explained I would pay the purchase price and his assignment fee. Wholesalers use the term "direct to seller" because they contract directly with home sellers to buy their houses, then "assign" the rights to that contract to investors who complete the sale.

The wholesalers add their "assignment" fee to the price to investors. Wholesalers have an amazing business model, as their top expense is finding the deals. Because they don't have to close on the houses, it's a great way to generate fast cash.

I did the math, and I was excited. This property could start me on a new portfolio of properties in a pocket I hadn't yet expanded into. I eagerly agreed to the deal.

I was new to my system, still working out the kinks; I didn't overfund as much as I should have on the front end, and instead just did a deal for the purchase price and closing costs. For that first deal, before I had perfected my system, I paid for renovations and holding costs out of pocket, but it still penciled out. I refinanced it and rented it for a great cash flow.

I had purchased my first property through deal flow.

Treasure Hunters

I make the largest returns on houses where a unique feature makes them a great deal—that four-bedroom house no one will buy because there's one bathroom, or the fixer-upper that comes with a thirty-day-or-more post-possession and just needs a little love.

This is deal flow. It's the ability to find a property and pay less for it than what others are paying for similar opportunities. Having a good deal flow helps build your cash-flowing portfolio more quickly and sets you up for success.

As you begin building deal flow, it's important to know your limitations. I run a full-time accounting and consulting practice, so I have limits to how many deals I want to run simultaneously. I've done up to four houses at a time, but that overextended it for me. I no longer take on more than two active projects at any time.

You should start with just one deal and see it through to the end. Don't bite more than you can chew at first, as you can get yourself into trouble. Get your system working, and then slowly and steadily expand from there. Track and obsess over your numbers and processes to see what worked and what didn't so you can regroup and improve on the next projects. Small, quantifiable goals are the only way to make sure you succeed.

Once you're comfortable and know your pocket, getting started becomes much easier. Be prepared to spend some time making contacts and learning the industry. You'll have to build time into your schedule for this. Think of it like a part-time job. It's unpaid for now, but it will have huge dividends down the road. In fact, if executed and structured properly, your part-time job will outperform the returns of your full-time, wage-earning job.

In little over two years, my small rental portfolio was worth more than $7 million and provided a cash flow of over $20,000 per month, not including principal paydown and appreciation. Let's say in a decent market the real estate goes up just 10 percent—that's $700,000 appreciation in a year by doing absolutely nothing.

It feels truly magical as it compounds on its own without requiring my direct involvement—unlike my accounting practice, where I trade my time for money. In my career, I sell time and access to me, which is impossible to scale past so many hours per day.

When your investments start compounding, they are sure to outperform—and likely multiply—your regular income and worth. And the more you have, the more it will compound.

Once you've decided what pace you want to go at, how do you find deals before everyone else?

I focus on four sources for deal flow:

1. Wholesalers
2. Real estate agents
3. Zillow/MLS leads
4. Drive-bys close to existing projects

Of course, you can find deals in other ways. But these are my main sources. Let's break it down.

WHAT IS DEAL FLOW?

It is the ability to find properties and pay less than retail. The speed of finding properties gives you speed in deal flow.

Wholesalers

Wholesalers are a great source of deals. Wholesalers are direct to seller, and unless you *are* the wholesaler, they are your best avenue to purchase.

Wholesalers pound the pavement for potential sellers. They do the extremely hard grunt work of sending out postcards, buying up pay-per-click (PPC) campaigns on Google and social media, putting up "I Buy Houses" signs, checking foreclosure listings, and even knocking on doors to find homeowners who want to sell. They run it as a real business and have tremendous costs associated with finding the leads. They cover those costs through an assignment fee.

When a wholesaler lists a property, the purchase price they blast it for includes the assignment fee, and you may not know much of what you're paying is for the house and how much is going to the wholesaler. Assignment fees are treated differently depending on which state you're in.

In California, you never find out the assignment fee; that information is protected by law. In Arizona, you find out when you see the final settlement statement. An assignment fee could be as low as $500 or as high or higher than $100,000, though typically they are in the $10,000 to $40,000 range. Wholesalers are experts in finding properties below market value, but only a few can be successful at it consistently. That justifies the sometimes high cost of the assignment fee.

When deciding whether a deal is right for you, keep in mind that the assignment fee is irrelevant. If the deal pencils, who cares how much is going to the property owner versus the wholesaler?

ADVERTISING TIP

You may choose to become a full-time wholesaler yourself. If you do this professionally, you will want to expand your lead sources to include paid sources. These include postcards, signs, cards, websites, text messaging, social media ad buys, delinquent-mortgage-payment lists, foreclosure lists, and just plain door-to-door knocking.

The Diamond Wealth Real Estate System also works for wholesalers, whether they want to grow a cash business or their own cash-flowing portfolio.

Homeowners who decide to sell with wholesalers typically do not have time to wait for a traditional real estate sale to list with a real estate agent, so they look for other ways to sell that offer more flexibility and speed. The homeowners can leave the place as is (not make any repairs) and sell it for cash to the wholesaler, which is why they are willing to sell it for less than retail value. These homeowners may be facing divorce, bankruptcy, death, job transfer, or other situations that force them to sell fast.

Wholesalers may or may not have the funds or time to purchase the homes themselves, so instead they talk to homeowners directly and get a house under contract. Once they have a contract, they assign their interest in the contract to a buyer. The wholesaler takes the assignment fee for being the middleman, and the seller and buyer benefit from the direct sale.

The top-of-the-top successful wholesalers who can perform often decide to "keep the best and wholesale the rest," but many prefer the short-term, one-time cash and funding of their lifestyle versus funding their portfolio. This works as a great advantage to you, the end buyer.

For instance, my returns on any given house I buy from the wholesalers will outperform their one-time short-assignment fee every time, because each house is a source of wealth and infinite returns. For the wholesaler, though, the assignment fee is a quick one-time income that sustains the lifestyle they are accustomed to. This works to our advantage as long as you have the system and process in place to take down the deals.

Wholesalers always are looking to expand their buyers lists, as a bigger list allows them to move the properties they have under contract that much faster. If you do enough business with them and they learn your pocket, they could give you sneak peeks before anyone else.

Keep in mind, of course, that wholesalers are professional salespeople, so you may not be the only one they give the sneak peek to. They sometimes do it to gauge the market and price, so be prepared to have competition on every lead. Remember that assignment fees are how they feed their families; don't take any of it personally.

Wholesalers also will want to vet you, especially if you're a new buyer. A wholesaler might not even send you a contract before you wire your earnest money to the title company. This means you're sending $5,000 to $10,000 of earnest money before even seeing the contract to secure the deal!

QUICK TIP

Do not get hung up on the assignment fee! If the deal works, it works. Look at the deal, not the assignment.

Where to Find Wholesalers

How do you find wholesalers? Here are some good sources:

- **Title offices:** Ask title and escrow officers. Wholesalers close their deals with title, so if you have a relationship with a good-volume title office, ask them for an introduction to or contact information for the wholesalers they provide services to.

- **Social media:** Join Facebook groups for the real estate industry. Twitter and Instagram are also sources. A lot of wholesalers like to showcase their success and have Instagram accounts where they show high assignment fees and the results (flashy cars, great restaurants, you name it). This is a great avenue for making introductions.

- **Postcards:** Have you ever found a postcard in your mailbox asking if you want to sell your house? A wholesaler likely dropped it off.

- **Signs:** Look for "We Buy Houses" signs in your area. A wholesaler likely posted it. Call and ask.

- **Referrals:** Ask anyone in your network if they know of real estate wholesalers.

- **Meet-up groups:** Join groups and attend events to network.

- **Real estate professionals:** Agents and mortgage brokers usually know some wholesalers.

I concentrate on two pockets in my market, and I use various sources to find tips on good properties. Most wholesalers blast their properties publicly, and others take those listings and re-blast them in hopes that their buyers list is better. It can be difficult to know who's listing it if you are not on everyone's list; often you will see two or even three or more assignment fees to various wholesalers depending on who brings on the buyer.

New wholesalers tend to have weak buyers lists, so they often will give the contract to a more experienced wholesaler to blast out. The veteran wholesaler then takes a share of the assignment fee or adds a premium to the original fee.

Some wholesalers can text you their new deals. Below is an example of a real one I received recently.

3 Bd 1.5 Ba 1,348 SqFt w/ 2 Car
Garage
Hardwoods, Tile Baths
Ask $110k
ARV $200k
ARV Rent $1,400/mo

Duplex Opportunity / Residential or Commercial
3 Bed 2 Bath 1,263 SqFt
Ask $85k
ARV $170k+
ARV Rent $1,500/mo
Txt 4 Code!

You can see that the ARVs look appealing, but do your own research. They're often inflated to make the purchase price look more attractive.

Sometimes, the ARV ends up being even higher than the wholesaler predicted, as you can see in the example below. The wholesaler predicted an ARV of $250,000, but after an appraisal, I discovered the ARV was actually $320,000. This made it a fantastic deal I quickly jumped on.

Wholesale price is based upon a quick cash or hard money sale net to seller price. The home is available for financed buyers however the price will change. Contact us for pricing if you are an interested financed buyer.

Favorable financing available for any property we sell. Inquire about terms and concession structure.

DEAL OF THE DAY

Wholesale Price: $175,000
Retail Price: $250,000

In accordance with your request, I have appraised the real property at:

█████████████

The purpose of this appraisal is to develop an opinion of the market value of the subject property, as improved. The property rights appraised are the fee simple interest in the site and improvements.

In my opinion, the market value of the property as of   March 23, 2022   is:

$320,000
Three Hundred Twenty Thousand Dollars

The attached report contains the description, analysis and supportive data for the conclusions, final opinion of value, descriptive photographs, limiting conditions and appropriate certifications.

I also follow a local wholesaler whose only model is to consolidate other people's lists. He re-blasts most of the major wholesalers' lists on his social media feed every time a new property comes available. This allows me to see a lot of wholesale deals in one place, even if I'm not on every wholesaler's list.

The challenge is that the second he posts, everyone else sees it too. I end up competing against other investors for the same property. Again, thinking outside the box and pursuing properties most others overlook will give you some advantage. Otherwise, be prepared to go up against the big guys and likely overpay. In a competitive market, you sometimes have to take what you can get.

Real Estate Agents

To find leads, make personal connections with the real estate agents who operate in your pockets. I don't work with retail real estate agents often, but from time to time I can get an off-market deal from them. Let them know they aren't the only one you're working with, but you'd love it if they contacted you first for anything off-market. If a house needs rehab, you want in!

Look for agents who specialize in investors, rehab properties, or fix-and-flips. They will add you to their list of people they alert regarding upcoming deals. Once you do your first purchase, they will start giving you better deals.

Zillow and Redfin

Another way to find leads is on Zillow or Redfin. You do this by using search settings: choose your parameters, including price, zip codes, number of bedrooms, etc., and the website will send you an email every time new listings come up.

Be aware that you have to move *fast*—within minutes fast—if you want to win the bid on free leads like this, because there's a lot of competition. You don't need to work with a real estate agent or have a real estate license to bid on properties. In fact, you can sweeten the deal by telling the selling agent that they can keep both sides of the commission, hoping that will make your offer more desirable.

Speed Matters

Whichever strategy you use—wholesalers, real estate agents, Zillow and Redfin, drive-bys, or advertising—you have to be prepared to move and perform quickly. Time is of the essence. You want to pay below retail price for your properties, or you won't get the return you need. The deal is always made on the purchase, but that comes at a cost, so make sure to perform quickly!

Anytime you make an offer on a property, you'll be in competition with someone. That goes for any lead source, whether it's a foreclosure list, wholesalers, or a real estate agent posting on Craigslist. You are competing with everybody—and this often means relationships come into play. Guard your word and relationships with everyone with whom you conduct business.

If you're seeing a deal on the internet, you can guarantee that hundreds or even thousands of people have seen the same lead. The person who posted the lead is being approached by tens or hundreds of people, each wanting to make a deal. The reality is that money talks. The person offering the most money will walk away with the deal—but with all the competition pushing the price up, it won't be the best deal for them.

Personal Connections

To be in the best position to get a deal, you need a first look at properties before they reach the public. And that means making personal connections with people who want to see you come out on top.

Do not expect to build those connections right out the gate. Start by finding a way to make deals work even if they aren't the cream of the crop, until you gain consistency and prove you aren't a one-off. Be careful not to overpay more than you can afford, but don't worry about being close to market value when you first get started, especially if it's a hot market. In time, the deal will always work out. Even if you tie up some capital at first, you will be able to pull it out eventually. With real estate, time is always on your side, and you will never lose.

If you tie up too many funds at first, don't worry—once you pull it out, you can do it again. And don't worry about missing out on deals; there will always be more, and it's impossible to get them all. Just concentrate on what you can get and what you can control.

Once you know how to create deal flow, the next question to ask yourself is where your private loan is coming from. Can you borrow it from your retirement plan, or do you know a family member or a friend with deep pockets? I will show you the money in the next chapter.

Chapter 5

ACCESS THE MONEY

"Good debt is a powerful tool, but bad debt can kill you."—Robert Kiyosaki

A Win-Win Deal

I have seen the importance of having a loan source from both sides.

Before I actively entered real estate, I once acted as a private money lender. A friend of mine called to ask if I knew someone who might lend him $40,000. He wanted a hard-money loan for the rehab of a remotely located mobile home.

I didn't know anyone, but I asked about the terms of the loan. I had some money in savings earning 0.01 percent interest, so anything would have been better than that. He offered a first-lien position on the real estate and a monthly interest of 1 percent, or 12 percent annualized return.

I thought to myself, "That's a great deal. Why pass it on to someone else?" Inspired, I offered to be his lender.

The $400 per month interest was great, especially since the money, protected by a first-lien position, made it way better than the bank. It was a win from both our points of view.

Around the same time, my wife and I were doing a huge renovation of our primary house (which, again, is always a liability and a financial black hole), and we had to liquidate everything we could to fund the remodel. I needed my $40,000 back, but I was locked into the loan term.

I approached my uncle Steve, who happened to be retired and sitting on a decent nest egg. Despite his great source of capital, he had no income or cash flow. After explaining why I needed the capital, I offered to assign my interest in the $40,000 note to him. He would pay me $40,000, and he would get the interest and the principal when the deal concluded. He instantly agreed.

That was the beginning of a fruitful hard-money relationship with Uncle Steve. The next time a deal came in, I approached him first to see if he had any interest in working with me as the capital lender behind it.

"Hey! Listen. I've got a contract on a great property I want to buy, and I wondered if I could borrow some money from you. I'll need $155,000, and I'll pay you 1 percent a month, with three months minimum. We'll have a six-month option to extend, but only if both parties agree. Are you in?"

Even though I knew that, because he was family, Uncle Steve would certainly extend a lower interest rate, I kept it at 1 percent. I wanted it to be a win-win for both of us, not a favor he did for me out of obligation. Because I offered him the going rate, he didn't feel like I was taking advantage of him, and he was happy to do the deal.

"I'm in," he told me.

Within six months, we had the deal refinanced, and I had paid him back in full. We both made a small amount of money, and we saw how streamlined it could be. That property purchase went so well that he's been one of my hard-money lenders ever since.

Your Initial Loan Amount

You have identified your deals and decided on your goals. You're ready to start building your portfolio. But first, you need to access the money.

Having a reliable source of hard money is one of the most important keys to making the Diamond Wealth Real Estate System work. It allows you, without any cash at hand, to purchase properties the bank would require a huge down payment on. It's also the only way to do the overfunded Cash-to-Buyer Twist.

When you have access to money up front, it changes the game. It allows you to move quickly when you see a deal, all while preserving your capital.

The first step to finding a source of money is knowing how much you need to raise—or even better, having a hard-money lender whose rates, requirements, and limits you already know. Since every house has a different purchase price and a different all-in cost, it is good to know what the investor's capacities are—it could be $200,000 at a time, or it could be up to or more than $1 million. Knowing the limits allows you to assess the deal and make offers accordingly.

You have to know how much you need to borrow before you make an offer, but you can't know how much you need until you have a property in mind. Then how do you arrive at that magic number?

First, look at the available deals. By the time you've done the work in chapter 3 to identify your market, you should have a solid idea about how much capital you need to access.

Then, figure out the ARV for the houses you're looking at. Let's say you find a house for sale for $190,000. You think with a little bit of repairs, costing about $20,000, the property will be worth $300,000. Add $2,000 for closing costs and $4,500 for holding costs, and your required loan is $226,500. Given that your ARV is $300,000 and your required loan amount is $226,500, the deal pencils.

Cash-Flow Calculations

In traditional housing sales, you would go to a bank and get a mortgage. The mortgage you qualify for would be based on your current income, and you would need *at least* 20 percent down.

With the Diamond Wealth Real Estate System, you borrow the amount you need, fix the place up, and refinance the property once it can fetch its top ARV. This means you can buy the property without any money down, pay off your hard-money loan, and get a traditional mortgage at a great rate.

I recommend overfunding your loan whenever possible, even if you have the cash to do it yourself. You can also create a note (a promissory note against the property) from your own entity. At the very least, you want to cover the purchase price and closing costs, plus a few thousand dollars to get you going. In the best-case scenario, overfunding will also cover the repairs and holding costs; your entire all-in costs are covered, and nothing is coming out of pocket.

It is difficult to overfund for renovations with a traditional lender, who will be hesitant to go over 100 percent. But with hard-money lenders and your own money, it's up to you how much you want to borrow, especially once you've done the math and you're sure you can pay it back and the deal pencils out.

There are three main sources for the money you need: your own money, hard money from an individual, or hard money from an institution.

Your Own Money

If you have assets, you can borrow against them. You can use your own capital as the loan, or if you can tap into your self-directed IRA, use that as your lender.

You can borrow against any asset, like a house you own or a business with decent equity. I met someone who borrowed equity against cryptocurrency he owned, which had a high valuation. Use your imagination and don't be afraid to think outside the box when considering your assets!

And of course, if you have savings, you can borrow directly from your investments or savings accounts.

If you have a self-directed IRA, you essentially have a checking account, and you can also use that as a private bank. I have a good friend who has a corporate job and a decent amount in his 401(k), but cashing it out was a terrible investment. Instead, he converted it into a self-directed plan. That gave him access to his money. The plan became his own private bank, acting as his lender, and now he has full control over his money and portfolio.

If you don't convert your IRA or 401(k) into a self-directed plan, you can borrow some against the value of the plan, but it's not as flexible, and the amount you can borrow is much lower. That may still work for you, so it's worth looking into both options.

Remember, it's critical never to borrow more than your ARV (what you think you can get to refinance the house). Stick to an initial maximum loan amount of 70–75 percent of the ARV, just in case the market goes up or down. If you miscalculate your ARV, you'll mess up the whole deal. You can still make it work, but if you miss on the appraisal and ARV, you'll have to pay the difference in cash. As long as you are prepared for it, you'll be in good shape.

Individual Hard Money Lenders

One time, I found an incredible house for $250,000 after all-in costs. It was outside of Uncle Steve's budget at the time, but I knew it was a great deal. One of my buddies was sitting on money in the bank, so I approached him.

"Hey! Listen," I said. "I've gotten really into real estate investment, and it's been going well. I think it'll be great for you if you're not getting enough from the bank. Are you interested in my next deal?"

I told him how much my uncle had been making as an investor and laid out the terms. Because it was a $250,000 loan, I offered a little less and went with 10 percent with a three-month minimum.

He agreed, and I bought the property. I renovated it, refinanced it, and paid off the loan within four months. To this day, I work with both him and my uncle regularly.

Individual hard-money lenders are by far my preference to work with. A lot of people have a lot of capital sitting in banks. These may be retirees with savings they don't need to touch for several years, new-money tech executives who just cashed out on a big business sale, or crypto millionaires looking to diversify into other areas. Maybe it's a family member who's done quite well or a friend from college you're on good terms with. Whoever they are, their money is sitting in the bank making 0.1–0.2 percent back at best.

You can offer them 8–12 percent annual interest, with a minimum of three months. They get a great return on their investment, and you both make a profit.

Professional Hard-Money Lenders

Professional lenders have very different loan rules from banks, but they can be tricky to work with.

They are willing to loan a lot more than banks, as long as they believe they will get a return on their investment. But with professional lenders, you're going to pay an origination fee, as well as penalties if you pay the loan off early. Professional hard money also has much higher interest rates—anywhere from 10–18 percent annually—so this works well if you're planning on flipping a house, but it can be risky if you're sitting on it and collecting rent.

Also, professional money will rarely lend up to 100 percent of the purchase price—and forget about overfunding the deal. They lend based on purchase price, not future ARV. The way you make it work with professional money is by taking whatever they are willing to lend and supplementing the rest with your own money or a secondary loan from one of the options I listed above.

For example, let's say they lend up to 75 percent of the purchase price; you will have to find the other 25 percent, plus whatever the overfund is, as a second loan. The second loan could become a second lien on the property; this can be your own money or maybe a family member's loan for the difference.

It is not as smooth as taking a single loan and overfunding it, but it's doable if you don't have access to the private lender willing to work with you and overfund the deals.

It also helps to have a relationship with the lender, as they will be more likely to see you as a safe investment. To build those relationships, find someone you want to work with and include some hard money in your strategy, even if it isn't the main source of your loan.

Some real estate investors have built good relationships with professional hard-money lenders over several successful deals. They now get 100 percent financing on the purchase price, but even then, they can't overfund their deals and take a loan out based on the future ARV instead of the initial purchase price, like I have been able to do.

The Diamond Cost Range

To determine how much of a loan to ask for, you need to calculate your Diamond Cost Range (DCR). Your threshold to make money on a deal should never require a loan of more than 70–75 percent of your ARV. That's the ideal DCR.

If you're flipping a property (which I rarely recommend, as it is just another job), you have more flexibility to risk a tighter DCR and make a little less money; you can overfund much closer to the ARV because you don't have to refinance, allowing you to be more aggressive. When you're buying a property to hold, you want to be more careful about hitting that number. The more equity in the house, the lower the interest rate on your loan.

If you can hit 75 percent or lower, it's a much better investment.

SHORTCUT FORMULA

All-in cost (purchase price + closing + holding + rehab)
= < DCR (ARV × 0.75 to ARV × 0.70)

This formula works no matter the listing price of the property. For instance, I found one property in a cold-blast email where the listing price was $175,000. Closing costs and holding costs came to $2,000. Add to that $40,000 for repairs, and the property was going to cost me $217,000. The ARV was $300,000.

I did my DCR calculations: $300,000 multiplied by 0.75 gets you $225,000, and multiplied by 0.70 you get $210,000. That meant my initial loan could go as high as $225,000 and still turn a profit.

Even if my math were off by 10 percent—$20,000—it was still a good deal, especially compared to the traditional way of purchasing. I opted for a loan of $200,000, giving me cash back at close of over $23,000, because I knew the repairs would be minimal, and I didn't mind having some funds tied up in the deal.

This is a foreign concept to most investors, as it flips the traditional purchase model upside down.

Reputation Matters

With each of these loans, different protections are in place in case you don't meet the loan agreement. A professional hard-money lender's money is secured as a lien against the property, and in some cases, especially in the beginning, you may have to personally guarantee the loan. If you're late repaying them, they will charge you a penalty, because they make money from their money; if you miss a repayment, that costs them, and they're going to pass that cost on to you. As well, you could burn any relationship you have with them.

For personal loans, reputation matters even more. You may have a contract with terms for what happens (and how high interest goes) if you're late on a repayment, and if you don't, you should. You want to maintain this relationship and treat it as professionally as possible.

Once you have money in place, it's time to learn how to get the deal.

Chapter 6

GET THE DEAL

"Don't wait to buy real estate. Buy real estate and wait."—Will Rogers

Cold-Call Email Blast

One day in October 2021, I received an email blast from a wholesaler whose list I was on, but whom I'd never worked with. He had a property in my pocket that checked all my boxes. The three-bedroom, one-bathroom property was in terrible shape, and it was selling for $175,000. I knew with $30,000 to $40,000 in repair costs, I could turn it into a four-bedroom, two-bathroom property, rent it for $2,400 to $2,500 a month, and easily refinance it at a new appraised retail value of $300,000 or more.

"I'm going to buy it," I decided spontaneously. I got the wholesaler's phone number off the email and put in an offer. Just fifteen minutes after that email hit my inbox, I had a single contract on the property, giving me an equitable title to it until it officially closed. For all intents and purposes, it was mine.

For me, the decision was easy because I knew my numbers and the area. What was the property's ARV, based on the area and the bones of the house? How much could I afford to take out in loans? What was the highest offer price that would still make me a good return on my investment? I can roll those numbers off the top of my head, which gives me the flexibility to move *quickly* when a good deal comes by.

To get the deal, every time, you have to know your numbers off the cuff and be ready to move on a moment's notice. Good properties move quickly, and it's up to you to pounce on them so you can build your portfolio and get closer to the infinite wealth promised by the Diamond Wealth Real Estate System.

How do you know which properties to buy? If you know your numbers, you can determine quickly whether to buy. If you don't know your numbers, you could pay too much for a property. You won't make enough profit, you won't cash flow, or worse, you will lose money in the short term. You can still make it work, but it is not ideal; and you can make it work in time, but you will feel the short-term pain, which will significantly slow down the growth of your portfolio.

To determine a good deal off the cuff in a matter of minutes, you need to know the following:

- After-repair value (ARV)
- Initial purchase price
- Repair costs and time to repair
- Rental rates

We discussed each of these numbers in chapter 2, but now I'm going to go into detail about how to calculate them and make sure you get it right every time. All the numbers work together to calculate how much you can afford to pay for any property.

After-Repair Value

The first number you'll need to work out is the ARV. We've discussed the ARV several times, but now you need to know how to determine it. This is the most important number to get right—or close to right—because you don't want to miss it and tie up too much capital at first.

To find the ARV, go on Zillow, Realtor.com, or Redfin and search for comparable properties that sold in the last three months. Then look at the current listings and see what is pending, as this will show you when properties are too high and don't sell well. Another stat I like to look at is how quickly the property changed status from "active" to "pending." If it is within days, it is a good indicator the market is hot and prices are appreciating quickly.

Make sure to look back no more than three months, so your numbers are as accurate as possible and the comparables can be used for a current appraisal. Don't just compare number of bedrooms or bathrooms, but also square footage, upgrades in the house (such as new roof, fresh paint, new air conditioner, pool, etc.), the neighborhood, and anything else you can think of.

I used comps to decide whether the ARV was accurate on a wholesaler lead I found on Twitter. The wholesaler had listed the ARV at $225,000, but the actual ARV was $375,000. Those comps determined this was a much better deal than it first appeared!

SALES COMPARISON APPROACH			
Gross Living Area	1,205 sq.ft.	1,000 sq.ft.	
Basement & Finished	0sf	0sf	
Rooms Below Grade			
Functional Utility	TYPICAL	TYPICAL	
Heating/Cooling	GFA/CAC	GFA/CAC	
Energy Efficient Items	NONE NOTED	NONE NOTED	
Garage/Carport	2dw	1ga1dw	
Porch/Patio/Deck	NONE	PATIO	
Fittings & Finishes	UPDATED	EQUIVALENT	
Auxilliary Unit	240 SF, 1 BATH	NONE	
Landscaping	NO REAR	TYPICAL	
Net Adjustment (Total)		X + - $	
Adjusted Sale Price		Net Adj. 3.8 %	
of Comparables		Gross Adj. 11.1 % $	

I X did ☐ did not research the sale or transfer history of the subject property and compar

My research X did ☐ did not reveal any prior sales or transfers of the subject property f
Data Source(s) COUNTY RECORD VIA MONSOON
My research X did ☐ did not reveal any prior sales or transfers of the comparable sales
Data Source(s) COUNTY RECORD VIA MONSOON
Report the results of the research and analysis of the prior sale or transfer history of the subject

ITEM	SUBJECT	COMPAR
Date of Prior Sale/Transfer	02/24/2022	01/05/2022
Price of Prior Sale/Transfer	$185,000	$323,700
Data Source(s)	CTY RECORD VIA MONSOON	CTY RECORD VI
Effective Date of Data Source(s)	04/20/2022	04/20/2022

Analysis of prior sale or transfer history of the subject property and comparable sales
RENOVATED THE PROPERTY TO ITS PRESENT CONDITION THERE WAS AN ADDITIONAL TRANSFE
INVESTORS PLANNING TO RESELL THE PROPERTY I CAN DETERMINE NO INFORMATION ABOUT T
DATE).

Summary of Sales Comparison Approach SEE ADDENDUM

Indicated Value by Sales Comparison Approach $ 375,000
Indicated Value by: Sales Comparison Approach $ 375,000 Cost Approach
MARKET VALUE WAS DETERMINED BY USING THE SALES COMPARISON APPROACH CONSIDERE
SUFFICIENT CONTEMPORARY PROXIMATE SALES OF SIMILAR PROPERTIES WERE AVAILABLE TO
This appraisal is made X "as is",

2bed | 1bath
720sqft | .16 acres lot

Asking Price: $185,000
ARV: $225,000

dropbox.com

2 Likes

Once you familiarize yourself with the properties going in your zip, you won't have to do this research every time; you'll have those comps at your fingertips. In a very hot market, I have seen other investors adjust the ARV based on future appreciation. That means they plan on the property appreciation while the rehab is going on, as it is three to six months in the future. While this strategy works fine in a hot market, it is aggressive and should be done only by seasoned professionals. If you go that route, exercise extreme caution, especially if you put yourself in a situation in which you need to hit that ARV.

DO YOUR RESEARCH

Some real estate agents and wholesalers will provide you with a precalculated ARV. Do *not* trust it! They often inflate the number to make the property more appealing. Use it as a guide, but always do your own due diligence. It's up to you to find out what the property will *actually* sell for. Wholesalers are salespeople looking to move the properties at the highest possible value, so it is in their best interest to present the best ARV possible. It may not mean they are intentionally being deceitful, but be sure to do your research and check the ARV you come up with.

Repair Costs

The second number you need to familiarize yourself with is the cost of repairs. How much will you need to put in so you can sell this property for what it's worth?

Knowing this number can be tricky until you have more experience under your belt. Talk to a contractor and get some quotes, or research house-flipping groups to find out how much people usually spend to do certain jobs. How much does a new kitchen cost? How much is paint? Some of these will be standard costs, and some will vary.

Remember, you're not renovating this for yourself. You don't need French marble countertops from Paris. You just want the property to be good enough for the appraisal to hit your ARV mark and then be rentable.

Again, relationships will come into play here. At first, your repair cost will be higher, but the more deals you do with the same general contractors, the lower the cost will be since you can give them somewhat consistent work. Once you've done a few deals with the same contractor, you will know the budget off the cuff. But at first, you'll have to talk with them to get a general idea of the range and find someone you can trust to keep to that range.

QUICK TIPS: OOPS BUDGET

Always build in a buffer of 5 percent of your expected renovation costs. During renovations on one property, I found out it had a bad main sewer. We had to dig up to the main and change the sewer line, and it cost way more than anticipated. A lot is unforeseen in real estate, and if you aren't prepared, it can have a devastating impact to your initial bottom line.

As a general rule, repairs cost between $35,000 and $60,000. You also need to include the holding cost of your loan. Hard-money loans generally have 12 percent annualized interest, which is 1 percent a month. If you're taking a loan of $150,000, that's $4,500 dollars in interest costs for the first three months.

You can almost always overfund to cover the cost of repairs on the front end, if you are confident that you can fetch the right ARV. If the initial loan does not exceed 80 percent of the ARV, you are in good shape. If it does, you will have to be out of pocket, for the time being, on the difference. Make sure you have access to the capital you need to cover the gap.

Rental Rates and Monthly Cash Flow

The Diamond Wealth Real Estate System is all about generating infinite wealth. To do that, you need to make sure your monthly payment after refinancing—consisting of your principal, interest, taxes, and insurance (PITI)—is less than your monthly income, which comes from rent.

To find rental comparisons, you want to know how much similar properties bring in as rentals. This research is done exactly the same way you figured out the ARV. Find out how much properties with similar amenities and footprints are renting for, using tools like Zillow, Redfin, and Facebook Marketplace.

How much can you expect in PITI payments? PITI payments change based on interest rates, so you want to structure your deal to work based on whatever rate environment the market is in. For a $200,000 house in 2022, PITI costs approximately $1,350 to $1,450 a month. If you can bring in rent of $2,500 a month, that creates over $1,000 in cash flow per month. If your PITI is $1,000 a month and your rent is only $1,500, you create a cash flow of $500 a month.

CASH-FLOW CALCULATION	
Rental amount:	$_____
− PITI:	$_____
Cash flow:	= $_____

For this property I purchased, my cash-flow calculation was perfect:

Purchase price:	$175,000
Closing:	$2,000
Initial loan:	$220,000
Cash back:	$43,000
Rehab:	$50,000
Holding:	$7,000
Out of pocket:	$14,000

Refi for infinite returns:

New loan from bank: $227,000 ($220,000 to pay off hard money plus prepaids and closing costs)

Payment PITI:	$1,287.91
Rent:	$2,500

My cash flow was $1,212.09 per month. Multiplied by twelve months, that came to $14,545.08 a year, or 104 percent cash-on-cash return in year one! That doesn't include principal paydown or appreciation.

The ARV came in at $320,000, higher than the initial $300,000 I calculated ($300,000 × 0.75 = $225,000 minus $5,000 in closing). My initial loan was just $220,000. If I knew it would be appraised at $320,000, I could have gone up to $233,000 on the initial hard-money loan, getting even more cash back at close.

I bought this property when interest rates were low, but even with higher rates it still pencils very well.

PURCHASE PRICE FOR FLIPPING

We have focused on holding properties and never selling, but sometimes you might want to flip a property, especially if you need some liquid funds to help with other buy-and-hold deals. If you calculate your DCR and it works, but your PITI and rental costs don't, you know that's a great property to flip. Calculate your DCR the same way you would if you were holding, but feel free to edge much closer to the ARV, as you don't have to worry about building in equity of 25 percent or more in the home. You also have to be extra careful your ARV is accurate, because you won't have time to build equity.

No Cash Out of Pocket

Most people will do a down payment on the purchase price and then pay out of pocket on the repairs. When you use this formula, you don't need to put any cash out at the purchase; the funding comes from the initial hard-money loan. If the loan is structured properly, you can even cover some or all of the repairs on the front end. The hard-money lender then gets paid from the traditional lender, making it a win-win-win for everyone, and you end up with a house and little to no money out of your pocket tied up in it.

About three to five months after your buy your property with hard money, you want to refinance it into a conventional loan. That's where the Cash-to Buyer-Twist comes, and you get paid to buy your cash-flowing property. How exactly do you get paid to buy? I unveil the curtain in the next chapter.

Chapter 7

GET PAID TO BUY

"The best investment on Earth is earth."—Louis Glickman

A Better Way

Before marriage, I wanted to get into single-family home rentals, but everyone told me, "You need to have 25 percent down and six months of reserve mortgage payments in the bank." I owned my own accounting firm and did okay by conventional standards, but I could not access that kind of capital. The barriers to entry seemed impossible to breach.

But I didn't give up. As a professional accountant, I had a good understanding of money and numbers, but I didn't know how to harness it to invest in real estate. I knew real estate was the path to the freedom I sought, but I didn't know a better and faster way for me to get into the game.

As you know, after we cash-out refinanced our first single-family house to fund a large remodel on our next house, I saw a chance to get in the game.

Finally, I bought my first investment property and discovered how to twist the conventional purchase model and buy with zero money out of pocket. The cherry on top was getting paid to buy properties. Deals are typically done at the purchase, so if you buy it right and trust your numbers, it will work every time.

In chapter 2, I explained how you can use the Cash-to-Buyer Twist to bypass the traditional requirement of 25 percent down, cover all your costs, and even put money in your pocket. But to get paid to buy properties that will bring you monthly cash flow and infinite wealth, you need to set yourself up for success.

Refinancing for a Payday

The first step on the road to financial success is the refinance itself. With this system, you will be able to overfund and pull money at the close of every deal you do. Sometimes that money will go to cover the cost of repairs, and sometimes it will just be closing overage you are pocketing.

That small payout with the hard money loan isn't your primary goal. Your goal is to get the asset and refinance the property, as quickly as possible, into a traditional mortgage with a major bank using the best, lowest, fixed-interest rate the market can bear. Within a three- to-five-month window, you should be able to complete repairs, increase the property's ARV, and find a renter into the home. You can then approach a traditional bank or mortgage lender and use the newly appraised value to refinance 70–75 percent of it, allowing you to pay back the initial hard money loan.

Whether your original lender was a hard-money lender or your own self-directed IRA, the new bank loan will pay off that loan, and your new smaller loan repayments will be covered completely—and then some—by your rental income.

Another perk of the Cash-to-Buyer Twist is that when you go to the traditional loan, your payments become fully amortized, often with an escrow account to pay your insurance and taxes. When dealing with the hard-money lender, you are responsible for the taxes and insurance separately. Since you pay interest-only payments to the lender, the principal balance stays the same.

Everything changes when you start having monthly principal paydown and cash flow, and you don't have to worry about paying the real estate taxes or insurance bills separately. You will be able to pay off your high-interest loans and replace them with traditional, much-lower-interest loans, all without losing a dime.

The end goal is always to be in a regular, fully amortized loan, using as little of your own capital tied up as possible. You're refinancing using a rate-and-term refinance, which requires just one day of seasoning, whereas cash-out refinancing has a higher rate and needs more seasoning. This way you'll be ready to pay off your hard-money loan as soon as the renovations are done, in one to three months. The interest on that loan is high. Paying it off should be your top priority.

A standard cash-out refinance becomes appealing if you haven't been able to overfund and you're out of pocket on the deal. Let's say you stuck $30,000 of your own money into the property. After a year, you want to get your money back. You cash-out refinance, pull your $30,000 or more out of the property, and keep generating infinite wealth from your rental income. It continues to generate wealth, even though your rates could be higher.

Since using the Diamond Wealth Real Estate System with my first deal, I've bought with a twist like this for more than a dozen properties. Every deal included no money down and cash back at the initial purchase close.

When I bought my twenty-first property, I was thrilled at how incredible the returns were. Just look at the math:

Purchase price:	$185,000
Initial loan:	$210,000
Closing costs:	$4,200
Cash back at close:	$20,800
Rehab/holding:	$55,000
Out of pocket:	$34,200
Rented amount:	$2,950

New loan payment at 6.25 percent PITI (the rate when I closed in 2022): $1,502

I ended up with a cash flow of $1,448 per month, which is $17,376 annualized, or 51 percent cash-on-cash return, not to mention the free $130,000 in equity. The returns are infinite.

I could cash-out refi it after six months and be in the deal with nothing since the value is good now. Or I could take 75 percent of $375,000, which is a new loan of $281,250, pay off the loan at $215,000 ($210,000 + $5,000 closing costs rolled into it) and get $66,250 back, pay another set of closing costs of $5,000, and be $61,250 cash back at close.

At that point, I will have all my money out plus some, and then the property will still appreciate, depreciate, cash flow, and all the rest.

Your Bankability Matters

Bankability is the single most important piece of the infinite wealth system—even more important than getting the deal or finding the money. I could probably write a book just on bankability, but for now I'll condense it into this chapter.

Bankability comes down to how safe a bet you are for a loan. If you submit your file to a traditional bank, will it believe you have the ability to repay the loan it's giving you? Without bankability, nothing works, and the model isn't sustainable. Being bankable is the hardest and most important factor.

A lot of wholesalers post on Instagram and other social media about the money they make and show their flashy jewelry and cars. Most of them are making a ton of money but don't own real cash-flowing assets. It's because no traditional bank will extend a loan to them; they are not bankable. Having great income without bankability is like a Christmas tree with fancy ornaments that is left at the curb in January because it has no roots to grow long term.

If you have a bad credit score or are self-employed and aren't sure how much of your income will count toward a traditional mortgage, find out how much the bank will give you in advance of making any purchases. Being bankable is a complex formula that involves not only a good credit score, but also good income and the ratio between income and debt.

Contact your mortgage lender prior to buying the house, submit your file, and ask them what you can do to be more bankable. Your mortgage broker is an extremely important part of your team. If the refinancing portion of the piece falls apart, you'll be stuck with a house on a high-interest hard-money loan, extremely difficult to pencil long term.

Contrary to popular belief, bankability is more complex than having a decent credit score. Your income-to-debt ratios, your reserves, and much more are considered when determining bankability.

Bankability for the Future

You must obsess over your bankability, because without it you will be stuck hustling one-time deals like flips or wholesaling. It may sound sexy generating six figures per month in revenue or more, but it is still a job, trading your time for money. It could be a lot of money, but you have to keep doing it all over again, month after month. It can't compound on its own, and it isn't scalable. Also, you have to pay maximum taxes on it. You can retire from it, sure, but it will not provide you with generational wealth.

In addition, you have to have clean tax returns with enough income to qualify you for a mortgage. If you're self-employed, add clean financial statements to that. When you are applying for a traditional loan, the bank will dissect your tax returns, financials, bank statements, and everything on your credit. All income has to be sourced, and all inquiries on credit have to be explained. You must maintain clean records to make it as easy as you can on the lenders.

Before you begin buying properties, get your financials in order. If you're self-employed, maybe talk to a great tax adviser or accountant to make sure they can get all your books and taxes in order. If you work for a company, make sure your tax filings are current and you have access to the files. If your credit is poor and you are currently not bankable, start working on it right away. Set repayment schedules and hit them every time. You don't want to go through life being held back by poor credit.

If you have multiple businesses or are self-employed, you also need to have clean profit-and-loss statements and balance sheets that tie up to your tax returns for each rental property you are trying to refinance. It may seem overwhelming at first, but if you have a solid foundation, it becomes much easier to follow. Once you get through your first refinance, you will have a better idea of the process and be more prepared for the next ones.

After the real estate crash in 2007, regulators tightened the rules, making the traditional lending process much more difficult. Since then, your bankability has become even more important. You need to have easy access to all your year-end income forms for several years, including 1099s, W2s, bank statements, tax returns, and so on.

Make sure you are extremely organized and have a great relationship with your tax adviser, as they will become your best friend—or worst enemy if you have a bad one. Your tax adviser can be the single reason you qualify or don't qualify for a loan.

ASK YOUR LENDER

Go to your local mortgage lender and ask, "What would it take for me to refinance this property? Can you give me a range? Am I bankable?" They will be great judges of whether you will be able to get refinancing on the property you want. No matter what interest rates are doing, to take advantage of the best possible rates, you need to be bankable, period.

No magic formula exists to bypass your bankability. If you are not bankable now, you need to become so as soon as possible. Otherwise, you will be stuck in your current place for a long time. Without bankability, you will not be able to scale your real estate investments, which is the only way to make the Diamond Wealth Real Estate System work. You certainly can't save yourself to retirement without it.

No matter who you are, your income, credit, and debt-to-income (DTI) ratio are key factors in your bankability. How is your credit? If you're self-employed, are you hiding income to reduce your taxes? Do you have huge credit card debt or student loans whose payments you consistently miss? Having debt is less important than making your debt repayments. It's all about reliability and ratios.

ARE YOU BANKABLE?

I can't stress this enough: if you are not bankable, I can show you how to make it work, but you will be missing out on so much. In my tax practice, a lot of people come to me and tell me they don't want to pay any taxes.

This type of shortsighted thinking will keep people not bankable and forever poor. Maybe somehow increasing your expenses and paying less in taxes seems like a good idea to you at first, but what if that one maneuver costs you a deal or prevents you from getting the loan?

Remember that taxes are a one-time expense based on income earned in one year. They aren't the end of the world if you plan for them, and paying them offers a world of possibilities and opens doors to infinite wealth and freedom. My advice is to remove that small thinking immediately and start becoming a well-structured bankable machine. It is the only way forward.

It may seem counterproductive, but your tax adviser and your lenders need to work as a team. Next time you are trying to avoid paying taxes, make sure it is in line with your big picture plan.

We live in the best country in the world, and it stays incredible because of the taxes we pay to keep up those standards. But most important, taxes are based on the income you earn in a single year. Just think of them as a one-time expense, an entry fee into something much bigger. And active wages (or self-employment income) are taxed at the highest rate. Once you have your portfolio established, the percentage of tax you pay will be drastically reduced or even eliminated.

Once you are livin' the dream, you can start borrowing against your assets and have a no-tax event, but you must pay your dues first in order to get there. It is a game, just like any other sport; there are rules to follow, but the end result is absolutely worth it.

The wealth you generate through real estate, including using this method, is wealth for life that you can then pass on to your heirs. Using this system can provide you with a lifetime of mostly tax-free income—legally! But always look at the long-term view, not just the short-term, one-time savings.

It is easy to fall into the trap of shortsighted thinking, but if you don't open your eyes to the bigger picture, you will be stuck right where you are, in that narrow, poor box.

Your Dream Team

As you acquire properties, you'll need to grow your team. I rely on my team for everything—I never leave my office anymore! My handyman takes pictures and assesses repair costs, my lawyer handles the contracts, and the renters come to my office to sign contracts and drop off the initial payments. This works because I have a team that knows what it's doing.

Your team should include the following:

- Tax adviser or accountant
- Traditional mortgage broker
- Handyman or general contractor
- Insurance agent
- Attorney

Your team will save you time, money, and headaches. You need to build a relationship with each member.

I knew a successful entrepreneur who didn't believe he needed a team. He handled his own books and drafted his own contracts, consistently generating over $200,000 per month. He lived a lavish life: vacations, fancy dinners, cars, expensive allocated bourbons, and splurging to impress lots of women. On the surface, and looking at his social media accounts, he was livin' the dream.

Or was he?

What he didn't know was that he owed taxes on all of his income.

The Internal Revenue Service (IRS) is a ruthless animal with seemingly unlimited resources and power, and his taxes compounded quickly. The interest and penalties compound daily on top of each other.

Over time, he ended up missing more than $350,000 in tax payments. With interest and late payment penalties, that number came out to over $500,000. He was lucky not to land in jail; instead, he ended up on a tight repayment plan for years to come. You can bet he isn't going to be making that mistake again.

There is no point on working so hard to build a great business with a rocky foundation only to see it crumble over something that should have been handled from the beginning. It's like building a mansion on sand. No matter how high you stack it, it will collapse. In the end, you will be worse off. Again, having income with no assets is like a Christmas tree that looks shiny for a season, but is thrown out in January because it cannot grow on its own. If you have income, but no assets, and you spend it all without paying your obligations, you have a sure recipe for total disaster.

If you want to increase your bankability, you need to invest in a really good team; don't go cheap on them, as your life and future wealth will literally depend on it. In my accounting practice, I know that when people ask me how much my services will cost, they're asking the wrong question. The question should always be what value will be provided; the cost is the cost and becomes irrelevant, but the value of the relationship will always supersede that. It is priceless. Having a strong team will also show lenders you're a professional and taking no chances, and it increases your odds of attracting the right lenders.

Without your team behind you, you're missing out on the gains. You may still be able to buy a house and flip it. You may even be able to rent it out while paying back your higher-interest-rate loan. But you won't be able to refinance for the lower rates that will allow the amazing cash flow you should expect from this system.

Let us look a deeper at your dream team.

Tax Adviser/Accounting Team

This relationship is one of your most important.

Your accountant gets all of your financials in shape and helps you keep track of cash flow and loans during the process. Make sure you hire a professional who has an in-depth understanding of both real estate and your end goal. They need to understand real estate, structure, and bankability. They also need to be a great team player who works closely with your banking and mortgage brokers. Make sure they are proactive and work toward your plan. You don't want a reactive accountant who just waits for you to show up with your shoebox containing a disorganized mess of receipts from the previous year.

Your tax adviser will often need to draft letters explaining certain items or confirming you are self-employed. Don't go cheap on a good tax adviser; it can make all the difference for you.

Not every accountant will know how to collect money, move money around, and structure real estate entities and deals. You need one who can keep your financials, stay compliant, and make sure your taxes are filed accurately and on time. They will also become a liaison with your banks and lenders. Often, lenders need third-party letters explaining your position, so it is important to have a great accounting team behind you. The accountant can handle much of the correspondence directly with the banks and lender, which frees you from the burden and allows you to concentrate on the deal.

Traditional Mortgage Broker

You want to build a great relationship with a traditional mortgage broker. You should be prequalified and "bankable" from the start. You need to know that you can refinance the house from the beginning so you can pay back your hard-money lender. Failure to do this could get you stuck with the house and risk the relationship with the hard-money lender. The mortgage brokers know your assets and liabilities and can advise on what to improve. Yes, they make good commissions on your files, but be nice to them and take them seriously, as their input is extremely important.

Handyman or General Contractor

You want a relationship with a great general contractor/handyman—someone who can do random repairs, keep the plumbing going, and fix everything from leaky sinks to small air conditioning problems. When scaling real estate investments, you don't want to take all the calls—you should be able to route your minor maintenance calls to the handyman.

Renovations are a big part of the success of the Diamond Wealth Real Estate System. You need to be able to get a house ready to show and come in on budget. If you're not an expert in this area, having a relationship with someone you trust will make all the difference. Overfunding can cover most or all of your repair costs, but you need to have the team behind you, or you will have no idea what those costs will look like. And of course, you don't want to do the work yourself!

Obviously, a relationship like this is built over time, but having them on board is priceless. Choose someone who's connected and can help you find other tradespeople who are reliable for the bigger projects they can't handle. And never go with the cheapest guy. You'll end up paying more for bad labor when you can't rely on your team.

Insurance Agent

And now for some not-so-funny riddles:

- What happens if a squatter breaks in and lives in your house for a week, clogs the toilet in the process, slips on the overflowing water, and injures his back?

- What happens if a tenant finds mold in your house, and their child gets sick from breathing it in?

- What happens when a neighbor's dogs end up on the property and bite your tenant or guest of the tenant?

- What happens when a water leak in the bathroom overflows into the bedroom, and the tenant slips and breaks a hip?

The answer for all of these is the same. Your tenant will see you as a rich, greedy landlord and will want a settlement or will attempt to sue you.

As crazy and horrifying as it seems, these are real scenarios. You need strong insurance to protect you. At all phases of your property, from rehab to tenancy, make sure you pay for adequate insurance. You can even add additional insurance on top of the regular insurance. You can never have too much in this business.

A knowledgeable insurance agent will make sure you're covered properly. A top agent will also save you money by having all your insurance under one roof and getting certificates of insurance for you in a timely manner when needed. This is an important team member.

Every lender also requires certificates of insurance, and the lender interest always changes when you refinance. It's important to have a proactive, quick, and knowledgeable insurance agent that can move at the speed of business.

Attorney

You also want to keep a real estate attorney or lawyer on hand. You can pay them as little as $1,000 or $2,000 up front, so they're on retainer. From time to time you may need them to act or review something, and this way they are automatically hired. They will handle the legal side of your contracts, including drafting the initial leases or coming to your aid in the event you need to initiate an eviction proceeding. Make sure they are also well versed in real estate and especially the landlord–tenant act for your state.

Now that you know how to refinance to buy and hold, we'll talk about your long-term buy-and-hold strategy.

Chapter 8

Buy and Hold

"Real estate is an imperishable asset, ever-increasing in value. It is the most solid security that human ingenuity has devised. It is the basis of all security and about the only indestructible security." —Russell Sage

The Right Call

In early 2020, I bought a house in Phoenix. It had four bedrooms and one bath, and I had big plans to fix it up. I was going to add a second bathroom, put in a dishwasher, and really improve the house's ARV.

A month after we closed . . . COVID-19 hit. I was struck by an emotion—fear. "What's going to happen?" I wondered. The renovation was a huge undertaking, but I didn't think I could move forward on any of my original plans. Adding to my hesitation, the government instituted a pause in evictions because of uncertainty about the ability of tenants to pay rents.

My wife said, "Let's cut our losses and just sell it as is."

I hated the idea, as I don't like to sell anything until the math makes sense, but at the time I let emotion take the best of me, and I agreed. We put it up with a wholesaler . . . and we didn't get a single offer.

We were stuck with our backs against the wall with no other option but to make it work. Sometimes that is the best thing that can happen.

I took a deep breath and thought it out. "Let's do a very basic remodel," I told my wife. "No dishwasher, no nice tile, just good enough to live and appraise. We'll get it clean and freshly painted, and rent it out with just one bathroom."

Shortly after the rehab was complete, I put the house up as a rental, and tenants were in place within a week. I went to the bank for a refinance, and they looked it over and agreed. To this day, we still have that property. It brings in over $900 in cash flow every month and has over six figures in equity.

All because we trusted the process and didn't walk away too soon.

We trusted it would work out in the end, and it did. Don't let fear get in the way. It is a natural human emotion that takes over, but if you stick to the plan and trust the process, everything works out in the end.

The cornerstone of the Diamond Wealth Real Estate System is the properly structured buy-and-hold strategy. While overfunding your initial loan and refinancing is important, you don't create infinite returns if you don't hold the property. You need consistent income to achieve the freedom you seek and build the life you dream of.

A buy-and-hold strategy also protects you from market fluctuations. What do you care if your portfolio drops by 25 percent overnight? The rent and your monthly costs are fixed, which means your infinite wealth keeps rolling in.

Buy-and-Hold Returns

In chapter 1, I told you the seven different ways you can make money from a single-family property:

1. **Cash flow:** This provides monthly money in your pocket after PITI payment.

2. **Principal paydown:** Your principal balance goes down, and your net worth increases with every payment.

3. **Appreciation:** The value goes up over time.

4. **Depreciation:** This gives you a tax write-off without taking money out of your pocket.

5. **Cash-out refinance:** This nontaxable event puts extra money in your pocket without triggering a tax liability. It's my personal favorite way to tap into wealth.

6. **1031 exchange:** Roll into more deals and scale your deals by deferring taxable gains.

7. **Cash-to-Buyer Twist:** Overfund your purchase and end up with cash in your pocket.

We can break these down further.

Monthly cash flow: This is the most straightforward option. It's your rent minus your mortgage (hopefully fully escrowed so taxes and insurance are included). When you look at a percentage return, instead of looking at the cash flow compared to the purchase price of the house, look at the relationship between the cash flow and how much money out of pocket you have in the deal.

As you add properties, the cash flow starts to compound. Your cash-on-cash formula, as described in chapter 2, comes into play. With several houses, you could earn total monthly cash flow from $1,000 to over $10,000 per month. When that total exceeds your wage-earning paycheck, you have freedom, which is priceless.

Monthly principal paydown: Take a look at the amortization schedule on a mortgage. What happens is that the interest is "front-loaded"; in the beginning of the loan, the interest payment is higher than the principal payment. With each payment, the loan balance decreases, acting as a forced savings method. Your net worth increases with every payment. This is a great reason to have a fully amortized loan versus a hard-money loan.

Appreciation: Over time, real estate will appreciate—period. If you do your due diligence and pick a good market, it will appreciate even higher than the average. Look for good market-population growth and high demand for single-family housing. In the early 2020s, America saw an even higher than normal appreciation rate, but even in cold markets, prices still slowly climb over time. Appreciation makes you more bankable by increasing your net worth without doing anything other than holding this asset. You start making money in your sleep; the houses are assets that compound and increase in value on their own without needing your active time involvement. Compare this to your wage-earning job, where it's impossible to scale other than hoping for a bonus or a promotion.

Depreciation: This is one of my favorite parts of real estate. When you purchase an income-producing property, you take a tax deduction for part of the cost for every single year you own it. This deduction is one of the greatest benefits of real estate: it doesn't cost you anything out of pocket. It is a noncash expense, and each year you can write off a portion of the property against the income. That reduces your net income and your taxes at year-end.

For example, let's say you have a basis in a property in the amount of $250,000. In most cases, 15–20 percent or so of the property value is allocated to land, which you can't depreciate. That leaves $212,500 to be depreciated over 27.5 years. You end up with a $7,727 annualized deduction against your income each year you own the real estate. The best part is that you can include the bank's money in the calculation. Even if you have no money out of your own pocket into the deal, you still get to depreciate. This gives you a great deduction against the income, as it makes that portion a truly tax-free income.

If you used the Diamond Wealth Real Estate System formula to purchase the real estate, your actual cash out of pocket will be little to none, and then you write off the depreciation on the full cost of the building, even if the lender or bank puts in the money! That's just on one property. Imagine ten properties with the same kind of deduction. You would have a total annual deduction of close to $80,000. This is totally legal and reduces your net income, so you don't incur any tax liability on it.

Think about this: you can have zero or little money into the property and take a full depreciation write-off against your income and taxes! This is truly remarkable. No other asset class in the world offers the flexibility of real estate.

Cash-out refinance: This is another incredible tool for generating infinite returns. It makes single-family residential real estate the most flexible and best asset in the world, outperforming every asset class—if it is properly structured.

In time, every property will eventually qualify for a cash-out refinance. Generally, you can take a cash-out loan of up to 75 percent of the appraised value at the time, or 75 percent lifetime value. If a property is worth $200,000, you can take a loan of up to $150,000 as a cash-out refinance. If your existing loan is $100,000, then you can take up to $50,000 cash out (minus loan closing fees)—with no need to ever sell the property!

If you sell the property, you will trigger capital gains taxes and lose the asset. Instead, take a cash-out refi if you need the money, and hold the asset. In time, you will be able to do this again and again, making it better than a traditional sale. The math works out the same as if you sold the house. If you liquidate the asset, between depreciation recapture and federal and state taxes, you will be at minimum of 20 percent taxes of the gain. Having a loan of 75 percent is similar to if you sell, but you end up holding the asset, which makes it a much better long-term investment.

When you refi, it's like enjoying fruit now, keeping the fruit tree, and harvesting more fruit in the future. After the cash-out refinance, you can still have monthly cash flow, enjoy principal paydown, earn appreciation and depreciation, *and* get a lump sum of tax-free cash. Again, there really is nothing like real estate.

Even if you have money tied up in the property at first, it's only a matter of time until you pull it all back out, making you a homeowner of an investment property with zero out of pocket. The returns at that point will be too great to quantify, making them infinite.

1031 exchange: What happens after you fully depreciate a property? Or you are sitting on a bunch of equity that no longer pencils for that deal? You're sitting on hundreds of thousands in equity, and you're still making the cash flow, but you could get more. This is when you want to look into a 1031 exchange.

Every house will depreciate to the point where it will make sense to move on to a bigger and better property. The 1031 exchange is a simple method of handling that. It's an amazing way of spreading your money out and putting the equity to work. You sell your property for a like-kind exchange, deferring your taxable gain: one income-producing property for another. When you do this, you're allowed to defer the taxable gain. And if the series of exchanges is structured properly, you can make these types of transactions in perpetuity. Never liquidate real estate. Instead, do a 1031 exchange for a new property or properties, which you can then begin to depreciate again.

Once again, you should consult with your competent

tax adviser, as it can get complex to calculate your basis on the replacement property and your deferred gains. Depreciation recapture, deferred gain, and other items need to be well documented. Whoever handles the reporting of the transaction for you must be well versed in the space and calculations that come along with it.

If you have a large amount of equity and are in a 1031 position, it may not be a bad idea to buy something that's already completely redone. A deal that didn't pencil before because you were trying to scale and preserve capital may pencil now. You are sitting on built-in equity that you have to deploy within certain time limits, so buying something that is retail ready at a retail price may not be a bad idea.

Cash-to-Buyer Twist: We covered the Cash-to-Buyer Twist in detail in chapter 7, so I won't get into a long explanation here. Just remember that this is the key to the buy-and-hold strategy that will build infinite wealth in your portfolio, as it is the best way to preserve your capital—at first. To start out in real estate, especially on a limited budget, preserving capital is extremely important, and the Cash-to-Buyer Twist is the best way to accomplish that.

Cash versus Cash Flow

Each of these seven paths to wealth is possible when you buy and hold. When you flip, you have access only to the immediate one-time cash; it's a job, which doesn't generate infinite wealth, as you don't own the asset long term. The next day, you wake up and do it all over again if you want the income. All you end up with is one-time cash, which triggers maximum tax, and frequently, you spend it faster than it comes in. It becomes no different from a job, as it is something you must do, and it requires your time, over and over.

Some wholesalers on social media post photos of their credit card statements, bragging about how much they spend to sustain their lifestyle and their business every month. It is always so funny to me that the loudest ones have great income but zero income-producing assets, and whatever assets they think they have are actually liabilities. The only asset is themselves, and without their sweat and effort, everything dies. This makes what they do no better than a regular job. Every month they are back on the treadmill, working hard to snag more deals.

Always value income over money in the bank, as it is way more important. Income is permanent, and in an inflationary environment, cash is the worst asset class to hold, making residential real estate one of the best. Your purchasing power goes down because of the never-ending printing of money and inflationary environment, and it doesn't give you cash flow.

In my opinion, the purpose of your money is to purchase

income-producing real estate assets that can compound in value on their own and bring you cash flow without requiring your direct involvement. This cash flow comes in, even as you sleep or take vacations. You shouldn't spend the cash made from a wage-earning job. Instead, invest it, and spend the cash flow from the real estate now.

When you add up the monthly cash flow, principal paydown, appreciation and deprecation, cash-out refinance, and 1031 exchange option, it makes real estate an unmatched asset class.

It is also a way to provide generational wealth to your heirs. I am a firm believer that real estate should never be sold. Instead, it should be kept, well structured, and passed down in perpetuity. Teach your kids the same techniques and give them the knowledge to do the same thing with their own portfolios one day.

Traditional schools will never teach these methods. Traditional schools produce good wage earners, not good real estate investors, and they have zero money education. You must pass that knowledge to your heirs and teach them about debt, how to make money work for them, and what true wealth brings them.

Mortgage Payouts

People holding properties often ask me, "Should I pay off my mortgage early?"

The short answer is no, almost never. I am a firm believer of leverage. You are locking up long-term loans at low fixed-interest rates to buy real estate, which will appreciate much higher than the interest rate and provide five additional ways to make money. The way to grow is through proper leverage. Paying it off could be the end plan, but it is not in the plans for anyone looking to scale or grow.

Also, you can do much better with the money generating infinite returns than paying off the low-interest mortgage. And don't forget that your primary house is a liability, so while you shouldn't mind paying off your main house, you should never pay off the income-producing properties. It is no way to grow a portfolio.

The math just isn't there, even if you have the cash in the bank. It's too hard to scale as you build, and the returns are much higher using proper leverage.

The following example uses a low interest rate, but the principle is the same whether rates are high or regular.

Traditional model with 25 percent down:

Mortgage amount: $180,750
House ARV: $241,000
Monthly payment PITI: $934.58
Monthly rent: $1,750
Monthly cash flow: $815.42

Paying all-cash model:

Assuming you had the $241,000 in cash and could purchase the house outright, here's what your math will look like:

House ARV:	$241,000
Cash out of pocket:	$241,000
Monthly rent:	$1,750
Tax and insurance:	$122.71
Net cash flow:	$1,627.29

Traditional model with 25 percent down and four houses:

Instead, if you can find four homes, each for $241,000, they will produce the same results as in the first set of calculations (times four). You would put $60,250 down (per house), and your numbers would look like this:

	Per house	For 4 houses
Mortgage amount:	$180,750	$723,000
House ARV:	$241,000	$964,000
Monthly payment PITI:	$934.58	$3,738.32
Monthly rent:	$1,750	$7,000
Monthly cash flow:	$815.42	$3,261.68

Using the traditional method for four houses, each with 25 percent down, the cash flow is twice as high, and you have four times the real estate, four times the depreciation, and four times the appreciation! It is always better to leverage properly for long-term infinite wealth. And it's all being paid off by tenants. This is just with the standard 25 percent down. Imagine if you implemented the Diamond Wealth Real Estate System—the returns would be multiples more!

If that's not livin' the dream, I don't know what is.

A Lasting Legacy

Once you own a real estate property, avoid selling it at all costs, if possible. Use the options above to access the wealth. Then pass it on to your kids. Teach them to do the same. This may be one of the greatest legacies you leave for you kids—cash-flowing properties and infinite wealth—but more important, they will learn how to do it themselves. Give them the ability and knowledge to take control of their wealth and their time! Traditional schools will never teach your kids this, so it is on you to pass it on.

It is simple. Buy and hold is the best and *only* path to infinite wealth.

Chapter 9

INFINITE WEALTH

"When you invest, you are buying a day that you don't have to work."—Aya Laraya

Lifestyle Riches

My wife and I started with humble beginnings. When we were first married, we had negative net worth. Our liabilities exceeded our assets. I had massive student loan debt, no real assets, and no way to generate wealth.

Remember our story about eloping for our wedding, and using that money to buy a condo? We used everything we had saved up and maxed out credit cards along the way, but we made it work. From our earliest stages, we knew what we wanted: to be a family with stability and the freedom to live life as we chose. But we had no idea how we were going to get there.

Real estate provided us with that life-changing path forward. We started with one property and turned that into the replicable Diamond Wealth Real Estate System, all without quitting our day jobs.

Now that we have achieved some of the goals we dreamed of so long ago, I see that while the money is great, the true benefit is the freedom money brings. This is what I've learned: always chase the freedom over money, and value cash flow over money in the bank. If you understand these concepts, your life will change forever.

If you're working a prestigious corporate job, maybe as a local law partner or an accounting partner at a big firm, you've got the money, sure. But you're also putting in 70–80 hours a week to earn your wage. I have friends who are partners at big accounting firms. Some of them literally have to bill an average of 45 hours per week, or 2,340 billable hours per year, to hit their targets. This doesn't include downtime, vacations, or time with family. The work–life balance is nonexistent. You have no control over your time, and your family will suffer.

Having money and income without the time and freedom to spend with your family—or in whatever way is meaningful to you—is pointless. Heck, when I started my accounting firm, I worked so many hours that I slept in my office several times per week during the busy season.

That is not the life I want. People get stuck and give up their whole lives chasing the dollar. They spend so much time working for the life they want that they have no time to live it. Money has absolutely no value by itself; if you can't enjoy it, then what do you do with it? You may have the financial freedom in theory, but not the time, which is way more important.

People think they're working hard so they can enjoy it all when they retire. In this mythical future, they'll finally have the freedom of time to live the life they've always dreamed of—except they get there and realize they're on a fixed income and can't go out and do any of the things they always thought they would. They think they will need far less during retirement, when, in fact, the opposite happens. Everything they want to do costs money, and there just isn't enough.

They have the time, finally, but not the financial freedom, nor age and health, on their side.

Nobody wants to retire and just coexist, wasting air and doing nothing. That's why you can't wait for retirement to start living your life. If you want to live the dream and truly maximize your potential, a well-structured, cash-flowing real estate portfolio is the best entryway to the game.

INVESTOR TIP

Value lifestyle over money. Value passive income with flexible time to spend with loved ones over active income with zero time for loved ones.

Thanks to the Diamond Wealth Real Estate System, I have passive income, sure. But more important, I have the flexibility and the time to live life the way *I* choose. No more working fourteen hours a day, seven days a week, coming home just to shower—or not even coming home at all.

With our Diamond lifestyle, I get to enjoy life now, instead of waiting for my retirement and starting to live only once I'm too tired and old to enjoy it. I still work full time in my accounting and consulting practice, which isn't going to end, but it is no longer because I have to. It is because I love what I do, and I have such great clients that we have grown together over the years. I get to choose whom to conduct business with—clients have to qualify to work with me—which makes me love it even more. Having the ability to say no to anyone with a checkbook that comes through my door is truly powerful.

My wife loves hot yoga, and she practices six times per week. It is her passion, and I think that's great. Back when I worked as a full-time accountant without any of the passive income, I could never share her passion with her. With flexible hours now, I often join her for yoga classes; we go out to lunch and enjoy each other's company. We can be involved in each other's lives in a way we never could before, and we have a true partnership.

This is all about the ability to control your time and money. Your reasons may be different from mine, but

they will transform your life too. I don't have any aspi-
rations of doing real estate as a full-time job as of this
writing, but I plan on continuing this path of growing
the portfolio. It is the best path forward for a regular
Joe who doesn't come from generational wealth. The
American Dream is alive and well, and real estate is your
ticket in.

You can do it now. With the Diamond Wealth Real
Estate System, you can enjoy your kids, your family, and
everything that comes along with that. It is way better
doing it now versus waiting until you are sixty-five or older
using the traditional conventional retirement model.

Your Diamond Wealth Portfolio

Start with just one house, see it through to the end, docu-
ment the process and your experiences, and go from there.
Figure out what went right and wrong. If you missed on the
price or you think you overpaid or sunk too much money
in on the front end, don't worry. A retail (bad) deal today
is a wholesale (good) deal tomorrow. In time, you will
absolutely make it work and be able to pull the money out
eventually.

Having the ability to be bankable and obtain good
fixed-interest rates with fully amortized loans allows you
to buy appreciating real estate assets. Those assets then
compound in value on their own and bring in cash flow

along with everything else. It is truly magical, and there is nothing else in the world like it.

Over time, you'll enjoy all of the benefits of infinite wealth, even with just a single income-producing property. Eventually the wealth, cash flow, and benefits your portfolio produces could be more than your full-time, wage-earning job, giving you the freedom you seek.

I have a friend who just started doing this on the side, and the equity he has created with just a few buy-and-hold houses far surpasses his 401(k) through the wage-earning job he built for over fifteen years. Again, real estate—unlike your wage-earning job—doesn't require your active time. You'll make more than you ever could in your working hours, all without lifting a finger. You'll stop trading time for a fixed dollar, and start letting money and wealth compound on its own.

In time, when you start 1031 exchanging, you can even move beyond single-family homes into small commercial buildings or nicer residential areas. Your options will be limited only by your imagination, and not by your cash flow. In time, deals that don't pencil today will pencil tomorrow. Be patient, trust the process, and it will work out in the end.

The Road to Livin' the Dream

Real estate has helped me escape the traditional mindset of trading time for money. I don't know of any other way for a traditional wage earner to start building true wealth and cash flow outside of their job and traditional 401(k). But now you know how to think outside of the box. Now you can have control over your wealth, your time, *and* your money.

As you begin to grow your portfolio, you are on the road to livin' your dream. Don't ever give up. Don't let fear stop you from taking the first step, buying that first income-producing house, and opening up the path to infinite wealth.

When you start walking this path, unexpected joys magically happen. That's how I came to own and name a street next to one of my rental properties: "Livin' the Dream."

Remember the photo in the "Introduction" of me with my street sign? I made that happen because a small side street, like an easement road, ran adjacent to a house I owned. The city decided to abandon the street because it was a dead end and they no longer had any use for it. No one owned or managed the street anymore, and it became part of the parcel next to it, which happened to be mine. I picked the street's name . . . and of course, I chose something that highlighted how great life can get!

On the path to real estate dreams, miracles like this happen all the time.

The path to freedom through real estate is yours to walk. Join me on the road to livin' the dream.

Peter & family livin' the dream - mid 2020 at the early remodel

ABOUT THE AUTHOR

Peter Diamond created and implemented the Diamond Wealth Real Estate System. In just over two years, he built a portfolio worth over $7 million that brings in over $20,000 in passive cash flow every month.

Peter's expertise has been nationally showcased on major platforms including Yahoo! Finance, Fox, ABC, and *The New York Times*. He is a seasoned expert in real estate; retail; fix and flip; ground-up construction; and long-term-hold, income-producing properties. Peter is also a seasoned CFO, a Certified Tax Resolution Specialist and Certified Bankability Expert™, and the owner of a niche consulting and tax advisory firm.

Peter has seen it all in the world of accounting, taxation, and real estate. His vast experience directly inspired him to create and implement cutting-edge tax, accounting, structure, and net-worth strategies for hundreds of clients, associates, and their employees. These custom solutions are aimed at minimizing liability, exposure, and risk for his high-level clients and top-performing wholesalers.

ACKNOWLEDGMENTS

Many people have made this journey possible.

I would like to acknowledge the best support team in town: Buzz and Danny, I appreciate you both for always being there, day and night, and bringing this dream to reality.

My great friend Alex Wilkins, who is truly the best of the best, definitely in a league of his own when it comes to wholesaling and buy-and-hold investing: thank you for your guidance, friendship, and of course giving me a chance to buy from your pipeline.

Josh Gayman, a close friend and amazing wholesaler who singlehandedly inspired the direct-to-voicemail marketing model and created the Cold Calling on Steroids system, which has been a bestseller for years: thank you for the early inspiration, friendship, guidance, and of course selling me houses early on, one of which gave me Livin' The Dream Street!

Another great buddy, the maestro of out-of-state real estate investing, Brian "The Lion" Tesar: for the tremendous support, friendship, ideas, and guidance along the way.

To Ilian "Skalata": for the continued support throughout the years.

Also, to the best hard-money lender in town, Uncle Steve: I appreciate you always being there and believing in me in from the beginning, starting with my very first deal. We wouldn't be here without you. You are as rock solid as they come.

To Helen Chang and Author Bridge Media: for making all of this happen. You and your team have been amazing.

The Diamond Wealth Real Estate System: A simple guide to building
a cash-flowing portfolio without quitting your day job

Author: Peter Diamond

Published by Livin The Dream Publishing LLC

Copyright © 2022 by Peter Diamond

All rights reserved.

Livin The Dream Publishing LLC
LivinTheDreamPublishingLLC@gmail.com

Limit of Liability/Disclaimer of Warranty:

Publishing and editorial team:
Author Bridge Media, www.AuthorBridgeMedia.com
Editor: Helen Chang
Publishing Manager: Laurie Aranda

Library of Congress Control Number: 2022915397

ISBN: 979-8-9860232-0-5 - softcover
ISBN: 979-8-9860232-3-6 - hardcover
ISBN: 979-8-9860232-1-2 - ebook

Ordering Information: